MW01226762

UPLIFTING LEADERS!
HOW TO HAVE DIFFICULT CONVERSATIONS THAT MOTIVATE AND
INSPIRE
Copyright 2020 by ALETA MAXWELL

ISBN: 978-1936839-3-77

Printed in the United States of America.

First Printing: October, 2020

DEDICATION

To my son, Markus. Becoming your mother made me view everything through the lens of living up to your future expectations.

ACKNOWLEDGEMENTS

To my dear friends, coaches, and mentors who love, teach, and encourage me. Thank you for your patience and support.

To my family, who have given me the strength and confidence from day one to not only go for what I want, but to believe I could be successful at it all.

To the original DT family. Thank you for allowing me to practice these leadership skills, for seeking my advice and wisdom, and being patient while I found my voice.

To my sister, Monica Outten, who is my original confidant, cheerleader, and truth-teller. Your help with this book has been immeasurable, and I can't thank you enough.

To Gabriel Capone, one of my first professional mentors, who believed in me when I could not, saw my potential, and had the patience and grace to help me to grow.

And, of course, Ann McIndoo, my Author's Coach, who got this book out of my head and into my hands.

Contents

Introduction

This book was written as a result of many years helping others have difficult conversations. It was written for anyone who manages others and must address issues they are uncomfortable with.

The following content will help those who struggle with finding the right way to have difficult conversations. Whether talking to peers, employees, or supervisors, my hope is that you become more comfortable with difficult conversations after reading this book.

As an extra resource and gift to you, I've created a workbook to help navigate personal growth in your communication skills as you read this book! The workbook is broken up by chapter and has insightful questions taken from the reading that will assist you in applying what you are learning directly to your experiences!

I suggest spending some time at the end of each chapter to reflect and answer the relevant questions in the workbook.

You will find the free workbook available to download on my website at https://upliftingleadership.com/about-the-book/.

Let's Dig In!

Aleta Maxwell

CHAPTER ONE

LEADERSHIP

"When you were made a leader, you weren't given a crown, you were given the responsibility to bring out the best in others."
– Jack Welsh[1]

Why am I writing this book? Great question. I have over twenty years of leadership experience and I can honestly say that I don't typically avoid sensitive conversations. I have come to the realization that I'm not normal in this view. I am consistently surprised at the lengths leaders go to in order to avoid hard conversations. *Most aren't comfortable having uncomfortable conversations.*

Throughout my career, I've noticed most people don't enjoy debating or having conversations which might take tact and forethought. Most people aren't even comfortable tackling something they don't feel they are excellent at doing. Communicating is something that has become increasingly difficult in this technology era. This ability to step into uncomfortable and hard conversations with others is actually a skill, not a personality trait, and sadly, not commonly developed in today's leaders. This is a shame as there are real consequences for not developing this skill and I want to share the lessons I've learned about communication throughout my experience. I believe many leaders can benefit from my experience and in turn, employees will feel valued and

---

[1] https://graciousquotes.com/jack-welch/

appreciated. This will slow turnover rate and ultimately save companies a lot of money. Learning how to communicate is a skill which all too often gets dismissed as being soft and only benefitting the receiver but not the companies' bottom line. I whole-heartedly disagree.

I'm fortunate that I was raised by two parents who loved to debate. I grew up around a dinner table where we leapt into difficult conversations nightly. As younger children, my siblings and I were shown how to converse on topics we were curious about but didn't know fully. As I got older and formed my own opinions in my teenage years, I learned how to have civil discourse on topics we disagreed on. My dad loves having discussions where he doesn't see eye-to-eye with someone. This set me up to be comfortable in uncomfortable discussions. I was also blessed with some amazing leaders early on in my career who took the time to further develop this skill set.

What's become more evident as I have gotten older is that many did not have these "practice sessions" at their dinner table, or ever. Most were not blessed with mentors who developed this skill in them. More and more emerging leaders are coming up in this age of technology, where difficult conversations are being pushed to primarily an online experience through email or text message.

Those who choose to develop out this communication skill set are those who have a much better chance of excelling in their chosen profession.

Throughout my time in Human Resources, the most common conversations I've had are with those who are seeking help to prepare for a conversation they anticipate having or those who have needed help cleaning up a conversation that went poorly. All these individuals had amazing skills that were valuable to the organization they worked for, however their lack of ability to communicate effectively held them back in one way or another. Since this is a subject I feel I excel at, I wanted to offer both emerging and well-established leaders my thoughts on communication as well as the lessons I've learned over the years. If you find even one thing I state in this book helpful, then my goal will be achieved.

I have worked in both the restaurant industry as well as in non-profits throughout my career. Many of the examples I offer will be from these two spaces, however, I feel they can be applied to whatever industry you find yourself in. My intention is to help guide those who feel lost when it comes to having difficult conversations with people they work with. I hope you will find this book helpful as you seek out ways to develop your own communication skill set.

ARE YOU A LEADER?

If there's even one person who reports to you, then you should start seeing yourself as a leader. This may be a scary proposition, or you may delight in this label. Getting to the point where we are comfortable calling ourselves a leader may take time.

Regardless of how you feel, if you are in a position where people report to you, it is imperative you start to see yourself as a leader and understand that your behavior affects others dramatically.

I often speak to entry-level managers as well as those entering the Director level who do not behave as though they view themselves as leaders. They are constantly looking to their own superiors for direction rather than seeing themselves as a person whom their subordinates look to *for* direction.

The first step of leadership communication development is solidifying in your own mind that you are, in fact, a leader. You have so much influence and a wealth of experience to share with your staff/team if you consider yourself a leader from day one.

A 2018 study published by The Work Institute states 11 out of 100 employees leave their employment because of their manager's behavior.[2]

> *How you treat people through your communication can have effects on morale as well as the bottom line.*

In this book, we will tackle how to communicate better to ensure your team functions well in order to have high retention of great talent.

---

[2] https://workinstitute.com/retention-report/

WHY GOOD LEADERSHIP MATTERS

"People join because of great vision; people leave because of poor leadership."
– Ekaterina Walter[3]

Turnover costs are directly related to poor leadership. A Seedco study published in April of 2017[4] reports entry-level turnover-cost per employee is approximately $3,300 each. The Work Institute conservatively measures the cost to lose a non-entry-level employee is more likely to be around $15,000. Think about what this means to an organization of your size. Think about the amount of money being spent to rehire and retrain individuals which could be going towards bonuses, training/ development budgets, and additional incentives for your team. This could make a huge difference for your organization!

Below are the turnover rates various industries reported for 2018:

- Technology (software), 13.2%
- Retail and Consumer Products, 13%
- Media and Entertainment, 11.4%
- Professional Services, 11.4%
- Government, Education, Non-Profit, 11.2%
- Financial Services and Insurance, 10.8%
- Telecommunications, 10.8%
- Hospitality, 70%+

[3] http://www.ekaterinawalter.com/tag/vision/
[4] https://www.seedco.org/seedco-announces-release-of-report-on-turnover/

The last number is correct. Over seventy percent is the standard industry turnover rate for hospitality.[5] That is a lot of people being hired, on-boarded, and trained who then leave for another workplace environment.

Regardless of the size of the company you work for, the costs of high turnover rates can add up quickly, affecting the bottom line. While some may feel there is nothing that can be done to mitigate these costs, I argue there is much we can do. Regardless of our level in the organizational chart, we all can play a part in bringing these costs down while retaining great people as employees.

PEOPLE DON'T LEAVE A COMPANY, THEY LEAVE PEOPLE

I have a friend, Robert, who works for a fabulous brand and is a brand ambassador. He loves his company and its' values because they are aligned with his own values. He loves what they do for their guests and how they enhance their guest's lives. He sings praises about the company and its mission whenever possible. But he's currently looking for a new job. Why? *Because his direct supervisor does not know how to speak with him.*

Robert's supervisor does not know how to appreciate him or how to make Robert feel seen or heard in any conversation. His supervisor gives partial information when directing and does not ask for Robert's opinion. His supervisor never verbally appreciates Robert. If his supervisor makes a mistake, he doesn't apologize or even acknowledge that he has made an error.

---

[5] https://harver.com/blog/causes-of-employee-turnover-in-hospitality/

Robert has gone to his supervisor's supervisor and voiced his concerns, however, there's been no change. Because of this, Robert is now looking to leave a brand he loves because of this one person, his supervisor. This brand is about to lose a loyal employee and a hard worker all because his supervisor doesn't know how to lead in communication well.

Unfortunately, this is not an isolated incident. Studies have shown this happens all the time. Companies spend money to find great candidates with pertinent experience and then spend money to onboard and train these employees. The investment made in each new hire goes to waste when they are tasked to report to someone who does not know how to communicate, build trust, motivate, or inspire them to greatness.

> *The number one way we can retain great people is to ensure they feel seen, heard, and appreciated daily.*

LEADERSHIP STYLE

It's helpful to be aware of what your values are and what type of leader you wish to be. For some of you, this might be very overwhelming. One way to start the process is to look at the leaders you've had in the past to see what values or styles you want to emulate as well as values and styles you do not want to incorporate into your own leadership. When I think back to the great leaders I have been fortunate enough to work with, I'm grateful to have learned so much from them. But oddly enough, I learned more from the not-so-great leaders. I learned how *not* to talk to people, how *not* to lead meetings, how *not* to tell somebody there needs to be a pivot on a project. I have witnessed what does not work very well. These experiences have taught me a lot.

You probably have a few personal stories come to mind when you think of healthy and unhealthy leaders. I suggest you recall these moments by getting still and quiet. Write down what your takeaway was in whatever role you were in. Also, write down what lessons are learned now about the good or bad leadership qualities that were portrayed.

Some questions to ask to trigger these memories might be:

- When did you hate going to work?

- What was happening that made you feel this way?

- When was a time you felt that you really "fit" with a team, and why was that?

- When did you feel your best at work, and why was that the case?

Get as specific as you can. Then, create a list of the leadership qualities you would like to emulate, as well as those you want to avoid. This will give you a great foundation to start with and clear intentions moving forward. My suggestion is to keep this list handy to use during times of high stress. The more you become aware of what good leadership looks like (or does not look like) and how it aligns with your values, the better you will be able to show up for your team.

I struggled with seeing myself as a leader when I was younger coming up in restaurant management. I had feelings known as Imposter Syndrome where I felt that since I was not an expert, I should not be the one giving directions or leading the team. This is because I had a misconception that good leaders were authoritarian and needed to have all the right answers. When I started to understand being a leader wasn't about me, but rather, how I made others feel, I began to get comfortable with seeing myself as a leader.

According to Tony Robbins, #1 NY Times bestselling author, philanthropist, and the nation's #1 life and business strategist, vital leadership values, traits, or characteristics include:

- Confidence

- Focus

- Honesty

- Positivity

- Decisiveness

- Ability to inspire

- Effective communication

- Accountability

- Empathy

- Humility

There are many different leadership philosophies out there. Many resources are available through books, podcasts, and papers describing these different styles of leadership. To find which philosophy resonates with you, first look inside yourself and figure out what your values are. Be intentional about figuring out what qualities you want to prioritize in your leadership. Once you have those qualities in mind, I suggest you read more about the practical ways you can commit to living these out on a daily basis.

Viewing my leadership style from the perspective of being a support to my team, rather than having all the answers, was how I became more comfortable with my role as a leader. This style is called a Servant Leadership approach. This leadership style has proven to be very effective in my career. It involves evaluating situations based on the needs of others and looking to serve those I work with. It is from this leadership perspective that I write this book. While evaluating the various leadership styles is a very important endeavor, this isn't one we will tackle too much in this book. I am focusing on the aspect of *communication* in leadership, but since I believe all we do in leadership should come from an intentional value set, even my communication guidelines come from a Servant Leadership approach.

While thinking through your leadership style, I challenge you to ask yourself how you can best support your team? How can you, as a leader, ensure your team feels seen, heard, and appreciated in order to achieve your goals and attain the best outcomes?

It is when our team feels seen, heard, and
appreciated that they will go out of their way
to bring their best selves to work daily.

FOUR PILLARS OF LEADERSHIP

Following my years of experience and hours upon hours of leadership study, these four words are the foundational leadership qualities I aspire to:

1. Uplifting

2. Inspiring

3. Motivating

4. Trustworthy

When I have worked for leaders who were uplifting, I showed up for them at work and strived to stretch myself. Uplifting leaders call others up, not out. They champion and encourage those around them and help their team believe the best of themselves. They help those they lead to see their own potential and then motivate them to strive for that potential.

When I have worked for those who have inspired me, I have absorbed their qualities such as courage, honesty, etc. I was able to do more than I had previously thought was possible because they were my example. Whether it was because they stood up for what was right or championed something I was passionate about or worked hard for, I was eager to follow them regardless of how hard the task was. When they consistently saw the silver lining throughout all the tough times, I worked harder and was more creative in coming up with solutions. I showed up for them and the entire team, not just myself. Even if I were not feeling up to it or was worried things wouldn't go according to plan, I gave my all for that person because they were inspiring.

TRUST

Trust is a foundational component to a great team, something which takes longer to build than it does to destroy and cannot be faked. Trust is based on action, not just words. Empathy and vulnerability build trust. Trust is also a two-way street. What I have seen in my own experience is *trust cannot just be given, it must be earned.*

When I trusted my leader, I was willing to be vulnerable, to consider when I was wrong, and to listen to their advice. I was more apt to give the benefit of the doubt.

Without trust, there would've been many projects that would have outright failed. We will talk more about types of communication that does or doesn't build trust in later chapters.

Trust is truly the foundation for a great experience in any team, whether it is the trust you have with your partner and family at home or the trust you have for your colleagues and superiors on the job. A great leader knows this and is motivated to build this trust every day in every interaction with every person.

How to Build Trust

As a leader, what are you doing daily to inspire trust from your team? Are you being honest and transparent with them? Are you letting them in on the big picture or are you just parsing out necessary bits of information so they follow you? I have found the leaders who explain only pertinent information have short-term goals in mind. They want to reach these goals as quickly and efficiently as possible and the more time that is taken explaining and answering questions of their team, the longer it will take to accomplish those short-term goals. These types of leaders want their team to do as they are told with no questions asked. The problem is, this type of communication in leadership doesn't build trust. *Great leaders know the long-term goal of building trust within their team is accomplished by taking the time to fully explain and welcome questions.* This type of communication to build trust is worth the extra time in the short-term and will pay dividends in the long-term.

One of the biggest ways you build trust is to ensure people feel safe and cared for. There was a popular television show a few years back that followed Cesar Milan, the celebrity dog whisperer. For some reason, it caught my eye one day, and I ended up watching a few episodes. Something he said about 'the pack' made so much sense to me and I believe carries truth for us humans just as much as it does for animals. Cesar Milan said that to establish authority within the pack or to be the leader of the pack, you had to make sure all the dogs felt safe. When the pack felt safe and protected, they followed the leader and were at peace. When they did not feel safe and protected, they did not follow but would actually lash out. Let me be clear: *I am not suggesting we look at our team as a pack of dogs!* But I believe there are many similarities to be drawn. We, as humans, also have the common need to feel safe. When we feel safe and that we'll be taken care of, we can let down our guards and collaborate peacefully. We start to trust more. When we don't feel safe, we keep our guard up, and we tend to lash out. *We don't trust those we don't feel safe with.*

Some ways to help those you lead to feel safe and show them you have their back is by not jumping to conclusions. Ask questions and be curious about information. When you work *with* them to find solutions rather than dictating, they'll feel cared for and the foundation of trust will be built. When those you lead know you have their back, they spend less time thinking of how to position themselves or "elbow" their way to the front. They know you will take your time and be thoughtful to include them in the conversation. When you do this as a leader, your team will be more focused on the right things, like doing their best job.

Another way we build trust is by being vulnerable. Oftentimes when people are in leadership positions, they feel the need to show that they are always right and in charge at all times. This is especially true in traditional corporate positions. But it's not the best way to build trust. When you show you don't know everything but that you're curious about others' experiences and opinions, it allows space for them to come forward and speak up.

I am a huge fan of being the first to point out my mistakes, especially when I'm leading a team. If I've made a mistake or forgotten to do something I had promised to do, I don't wait for someone else to call me out on it. I raise my hand and call myself out, clearly, in front of the group. This shows to my team the behavior of being vulnerable is expected, and it also builds trust as it shows that I will own up to my mistakes even if it's uncomfortable. It's okay to fail or mess up. It's okay to make mistakes because we are human. This is just part of the human experience, and by allowing others to see you admit this will set the tone and culture for the entire group.

There are many ways to verbally take responsibility when you know you have made a mistake. Examples of what this might sound like would be, "Hey guys, the schedule I posted yesterday – whew! I don't know what I was thinking, but I need to redo that one. I'm so sorry." Or, "I just realized I dropped the ball and didn't send the email out that I said I would. I am so sorry! I'll make sure to get this done immediately." It can be that simple. You don't have to give a long, drawn-out story explaining why the task wasn't completed or all the ways your mistake impacted the team. Simply stating there was an error, apologizing for the impact, and guaranteeing to correct it going forward is all that's needed.

Any time I've had a leader who did this, I automatically trusted them more. I then went on to give them the benefit of the doubt and even felt more comfortable pointing out errors going forward, knowing my supervisor wasn't going to get defensive but own the mistake quickly and correct it.

Oftentimes, especially with newer managers, I see there is a tendency to think they need to know everything and admitting they do not will be seen as a sign of weakness. I would pose it is, in fact, just the opposite. When the person in charge admits to not knowing everything, is open to hearing different perspectives, and tapping into the knowledge of the group, then this leader is showing strength. This leader is confident in what they bring to the table, and it is this confidence through inclusion, along with a large dose of hustle/hard work, which will allow them to lead their team through more turbulent times.

Showing empathy is a huge trust builder. When you show that you are interested in how another person feels, it builds the relationship with trust. Even to share when you've made mistakes similar to theirs and how you've grown from those times allows for connection with each other which builds trust. These are great ways to lead without directing. They will learn from your own pitfalls and hopefully avoid them. When you're able to be vulnerable and show you are an imperfect being who is still learning and growing, it allows others the ability to relate with you and this establishes trust. At the end of the day, your team's ability to see you as a human and not an all-knowing robot will be a long-term asset. They are going to see you as someone who is transparent. This translates to a lot more grace given when you do make a mistake.

Making a mistake is what humans do. Without a doubt, you will make many throughout your career. When these mistakes happen, we hope others will give us the benefit of the doubt, allow us to course-correct, and the opportunity to grow from it. When giving the benefit of the doubt becomes a part of our team culture, so many stumbling blocks will be avoided. Assumptions will not be made but space will be given for the offending party to voice their intention as well as own their mistakes. This benefit of the doubt and space given for dialogue will avoid many hurt feelings which could lead to resentment.

I once had an employee, Paul, come to me wanting to transfer from the restaurant he was at to another location. When I asked why, he told me it was because his manager was *always* messing up his schedule. After several minutes of asking further questions of specifics, I gathered that when Paul was hired, he let his manager know he could not work Fridays. This seemed to be honored for some time, however, the last four Fridays he'd been scheduled. When asked if he spoke up about this scheduling issue, Paul answered, "No, he knows what my availability is." I implored him to give the benefit of the doubt and asked if he would be comfortable talking to his manager about this. I coached him on how to bring this up and how he could describe to his manager that this issue made him feel unvalued at work.

A few days later I stopped into Paul's location to follow up. Sure enough, when I asked how the conversation went, Paul relayed that the manager was shocked at how he felt and let him know he had just completely forgotten Paul was not available on Fridays. The manager also asked Paul why he did not immediately point out this mistake so it could be corrected. This led to a great discussion where Paul could see that his manager was human and prone to human error. Paul realized his manager's intentions were not to dishonor the availability Paul had initially given him.

My follow-up with the manager revealed that he came away from the discussion with a renewed dedication to check in with specific questions of his employees to ensure that all was, in fact, good. If he, as a manager, asked specific questions of Paul, such as, "How do you feel about your schedule?" or "Is there anything I could do better?" the issue might have been avoided.

How many times has this happened to us? Our boss makes a mistake and we sit there and think they did it on purpose. We think they must have done whatever it was to punish or to send a message. Often, these assumptions happen because a relationship built on trust had not been established, therefore we don't feel comfortable speaking up right away. Once you build trust with someone, you are more inclined to think a mistake is not deliberate, but rather, just an error. When we take the time to build trust with our team, we get to then spend time focusing on issues which need our attention, rather than spending time undoing the false narratives that have been built off of assumptions based on lack of trust.

Thinking back over my career, it is when I have trusted a leader and felt inspired by her/him in an uplifting way that I have been motivated to take on the tough project or go the extra mile for the team's goals. When I am being led by someone who lives out these qualities, I show up consistently with my best self. Therefore, I go back to these four pillars time and time again as the base for my leadership.

CHAPTER TWO

SEEN, HEARD AND APPRECIATED

"Success in business is all about people: take care of them and they will take care of the business."
– Richard Branson[6]

INTENTION AND IMPACT

As a leader, you have an opportunity to see your people for who they are and who they want to be, to hear them, and make them feel appreciated on a daily basis. There are hundreds of opportunities to do this *DAILY!*

In every conversation, my intention is to ensure the other person is feeling seen, heard, and appreciated. I set this as my intention because I want the impact of the conversation to be much more than just an agreement of a solution. The goal of the conversation might be to solve a problem or deal with an issue, but my intention of the conversation is to ensure my team feels seen, heard, and appreciated.

It does no good to set my intention as accomplishing short-term goals if the impact of the conversation damages trust and the relationship.

---

[6] https://www.facebook.com/RichardBranson/posts/success-in-business-is-all-about-people-take-care-of-them-theyll-take-care-of-bu/10155011322005872/

TRANSACTIONAL CONVERSATIONS VS TRANSFORMATIONAL CONVERSATIONS

A transactional conversation simply states what the problem is with either the solution and/or penalty. Then, usually, the conversation ends. We want to avoid transactional conversations as much as possible.

If you, as a leader, choose to have mostly transactional conversations in place of deeper conversations, I guarantee your turnover costs will rise and your retention will go down. These types of conversations make employees feel like a number. Nobody wants to feel like a number. If your intention is to make sure they feel seen, heard, and appreciated then you cannot rely solely on transactional conversations.

Throughout your busy day, you will have transactional moments with your team. Giving directives and feedback can, at times, be quick and transactional. When you are having a conversation, especially a difficult one, the intent should be to have one that is more transformational rather than transactional.

Transformational conversations look to accomplish deep-rooted change by seeking to understand the root cause of the problem as well as collaborate on a long-lasting solution. When we aim to have transformational conversations with our team, those with the purpose to enact lasting change, we will start to see a difference in our team's performance. When you simply have transactional conversations, you will find yourself having similar conversations repeatedly because these tend to not look deeper than the surface issue.

A way to avoid transactional conversations is to keep in mind you don't know everything and invite expertise or opinions from others. Just because someone does not have a fancy title does not mean they cannot contribute to finding an essential solution for the team. Our employees are sometimes the best people to bring us new information or new ways of doing things. Be open to taking great ideas from wherever they come from and allow the contributions of the team to aid in reaching the overall goal.

If you walk away and cannot explain why the problems occurred in the first place, or why someone felt the way they did, then chances are you've had a transactional conversation.

Let me tell you about David and Sarah. Sarah, the manager, noticed that David had been "off" for a while. He used to come into the office a little early, super upbeat and was on top of his projects. Lately, he has been coming in exactly on time or even a bit late, seems to keep to himself, and has been dropping the ball on several projects.

Sarah tells her boss that she's decided to address the issue with David. Sarah and David meet and have a fifteen-minute conversation. Sarah reports back to her boss the conversation went well, and she believes David will make sure to stay on top of his projects going forward. Sarah's boss asks her why David has been off of his game and what the reason was for the project issues. Sarah cannot explain why.

Turns out that Sarah only spoke to David about the projects and simply wanted to ensure there were no more balls dropped moving forward. What do you think the outcome will be from this conversation? The root cause was not spoken about or dealt with. Do you think this issue has been addressed satisfactorily? Or do you think there will probably be another conversation in David and Sarah's future? My money is on the latter. Sarah had a conversation to tell David what she wanted, rather than to hear from David about what was going on with him. Do not leave the conversation unless you know the why.

If our intention is to build a connection with our team and to make sure they feel seen, heard, and appreciated, then the more transactional conversations we have with our team members, our peers, and our supervisors, the less we build connection and the less our team will feel valued. We will discuss more about how to have transformational conversations in later chapters.

FEELING SEEN

As I've stated, earlier in my tenure as a Senior Leader, I was not as comfortable with my own leadership authority. I worked for a company that had multiple restaurant locations separate from our office that I would often visit to counsel, investigate an issue, or follow-up with a previous conversation. When I walked into a restaurant, I would go directly to the person I was there to meet with, not saying "hello" to very many people along the way.

In my mind, I was not anybody special, so why would anyone want to say "hi" to me? My intention was to not disturb others while they worked, but I did not understand the role I played in the company and how this might be perceived. I am exceedingly grateful a colleague pulled me aside to let me know how I was perceived by others. I was shocked to hear the team felt that I did not value them by not saying "hello". I was mortified to hear they felt I did not think they were important enough for me to take the time to greet them. This was the opposite of how I felt! I realized that because I was a leader in the company, stopping to greet others made them feel valued and seen. This was not about how I was viewed personally, but rather, because of my position of power and authority, was way more about how the employees saw themselves.

This was a great moment of learning for me, and one that did end up changing how I viewed leadership. My colleague knew that having a hard conversation with me in the right way was possibly going to be an asset in my professional life! I resolved then and there to take the time to say "hello" to each person, look them in their eyes, ask how they're doing, and wait for the answer, whenever I entered a new location. I want to ensure everyone I work with knows how important they are to me, how much I appreciate the work they do, and that I am there for them. It is why I started learning more about the Servant Leadership philosophy, which ended up impacting every area of my professional life. Keeping the values of this approach in mind and creating habits that are aligned to these values helps make sure my actions lead each team member to feel more seen, heard, and appreciated. Keeping this approach and its values solidified in my mind allows me to always come back to my center in times of uncertainty.

This learning opportunity allowed me to share with others as well. Not long after this incident, I was setting up an orientation day for new managers to meet with department heads at our office. Sure enough, one of the leaders in our organization, Marie, asked me why I thought it was so important for the team of new managers to meet with her. "Who am I to take their time?" was the tenement of her question. I shared with her my story and lessons learned, then asked Marie to change her perspective to one which views the meeting as an opportunity to add value by showing the new team members how she can support them. She appreciated me sharing this perspective and ended up putting together a great segment the managers loved. She shared with them all the ways her department could support them and make their jobs easier. Taking her ego out of the equation and shifting her mindset to question how she can help and support, allowed Marie to go above and beyond to connect with and help the team as a unit.

Once Marie started to see that this is about the team, specifically the team's needs, viewing it from the servant leadership approach, she understood she was here to be a leader which does not always mean the star of the show. It was about the uplifting and growth of those she was leading.

FEELING HEARD

Another way to increase employee engagement is to strive to ensure our staff/employees feel heard. All too often I hear from clients that they simply do not feel heard or their supervisor does not listen to them. Usually, the case is that their supervisor or manager assumes to know what the problem or the situation is about, but really, they do not.

> *Relying on assumptions without asking questions or seeking more information ends up wasting time and hurting feelings. Both are hard to undo.*

ASKING QUESTIONS

One common complaint in the restaurant industry is how some managers close a restaurant for the night. The tasks associated with closing a restaurant properly are typically written down, and managers are usually trained in this area. Still, there are times when the general manager will open the restaurant the next day and find that the previous night's closing manager did not follow the given plan.

Often, the complaint is that numerous tasks were not done or not done properly, creating more work to open the next day. During my time in human resources, this situation was usually brought to me when the general manager was at their breaking point and were fed up with their closing manager. The first thing I always asked was how did their conversation go? Many times, the "conversation" was a one-way conversation. Usually, the general manager would tell the closing manager what went wrong, without any inquiries as to why it happened. I would typically share the following scenario with them. I would ask them to imagine they walked in to open the restaurant in the morning and found it a mess. Instead of letting their frustrations take hold, what if they wrote down what was not done and prepared to have a conversation. When the assistant manager who did the closing comes in for the day, the general manager asks them to sit down for a conversation. During the conversation, the general manager could communicate they were disappointed in how the restaurant was left and ask to be walked through what might have gone wrong. It is amazing what can be uncovered if you refuse to blame in the moment, but simply ask questions out of curiosity to solve a problem.

Often, this initial inquiry and the follow-up questions uncover issues not apparent on the outset. In my experience, there could be staffing issues, time management issues, deployment issues, scheduling issues, or training issues.

When you get to the root cause of the problem, you can help solve and come up with solutions together. This unearthing of issues and solutions would never happen if we assume that it is just a matter of poor performance. If leaders rely on assumptions and follow-up with one-way conversations then, most likely, resentment and possible turnover of good employees will result. If we, as leaders, do not take the time to ask questions and listen to our team, many undesirable outcomes will continue to take place.

I have found that very few people go to work to do a poor job. But so often, people lack resources and training or simply aren't great at coming up with creative solutions to the problems at hand. This is where you, as the leader, come in!

> *It is your responsibility, as a leader, to ask questions, help come up with creative solutions, and work out a plan to implement them as a team. Developing these skills is how you can add immense value to an organization.*

Making sure our employees feel heard is a foundation for building trust. It is universal that we all want to feel seen, heard, and appreciated. If your goal is to ensure you accomplish this throughout your conversations then the energy you present, the words you choose, and the final solution will be rooted in these intentions. Let the person you are talking with know you have heard and understood them by reflecting their feelings and thoughts. You may not agree, however that is not the goal. Allowing them to know that you hear them is huge. Therefore, step one must be to listen. Once you hear what they are feeling and thinking, it is often helpful to check with them to see if you've heard them correctly. Reflect back to them what you have heard. For example, this kind of reflecting question could be, "What I'm hearing you say is you are frustrated by the way the communication has been lately, is that correct?" You are not stating that you agree. You are not promising any specific action or solution. You are simply confirming you have heard them correctly. By reflecting back to them what you have heard and allowing them the opportunity to correct misinterpretations, you are communicating you value what they have to say. They will feel heard.

Once this pattern of communication has been established, they are more apt to truly hear you with the same focus and attention. We cannot ask for anyone to spend time and energy listening to us if we will not offer that of ourselves. Remember to check in with them throughout the conversation by reiterating what they are saying. This not only helps your team feel heard and valued but is the most efficient way to clear up problems and resolve issues. Developing this reflecting skill will help avoid many misinterpretations and therefore wasted time. Intentional listening is more than just verbal communication.

Paying attention to body language, energy, and non-verbal cues is also very important. If you come to the end of a conversation with an agreed-upon solution, however, the other person's non-verbal cues are saying they are still upset, they are telling you they are not satisfied with the resolution. If you get up right then and walk away, you will be sitting back down to speak with them again soon. Instead of rushing the end of the conversation because you have a verbal agreement, I invite you to simply state what you are seeing in their non-verbal cues. State that you feel their energy is telling you they are still not happy. Let them know you are listening to them through their body language and that you want to ensure the agreed-upon solution meets their goals. Intentional listening means using our ears to hear someone's words but also using our other senses and paying attention to what they are communicating to you through non-verbal cues as well.

Intentional listening means that you are giving them your full attention. You are facing them, looking at them in the eye, and truly focusing your attention on them. This is crucial, as it not only symbolizes respect but will allow you to tune-in to the various non-verbal communication that is happening. Their body language and energy will not be read by you if you are not giving full attention.

Difficult conversations are a way to not only solve problems or mitigate issues that arise, but they are unique opportunities to learn, build trust, and develop for all parties involved. Do not miss out on these opportunities!

FEELING APPRECIATED

DEPOSITS INTO THE 'GOOD WILL BANK'

People not only want to be seen and heard, but they want to be seen and heard in specific ways. Get curious about this. Learn how your team feels appreciated and valued. Appreciation and encouragement are beautiful ways to let your team/staff know they are valued. If you feel you are truly seeing them for who they are, then speak to this.

Acknowledge that you see them for the hard work they do. Acknowledge that you see the growth they have made recently or even their vulnerability in conversations.

Appreciating people in the moment is a way you can build goodwill and establish trust with others. When you see something you like, maybe a report done well or someone going out of their way for another person, point it out right then and there. Acknowledge those small moments, as we all need to feel appreciated to be able to do our best work. Every time you go out of your way for another, whether that is helping out on a project, helping them to finish their duties for the day, or verbally acknowledging their good work, it is a deposit into the Good Will Bank.

As one of my colleagues used to say, the more deposits you make into this Good Will Bank, the more you have available to withdraw from when the time comes to have difficult conversations and/or need employees to go above and beyond. If you are generous with the recognition, praise, and encouragement, then when you need to point out areas of growth, your comments will not feel like huge blows, but rather just feedback in the moment.

I have seen when managers are constantly giving both positive and negative feedback, then both appreciation and learning are constantly taking place. This will lead to more engaged employees. Comparatively, when only negative feedback is given, employees feel like they are not appreciated and valued and begin to check out mentally.

This type of constant verbal positive feedback for even small achievements is at first very awkward to begin to implement. It is not the norm in the workplace today and will seem weird. This is a habit that takes practice as a leader to feel normal and easy, however, it is a worthwhile habit to start. This practice is contagious and will create a culture of appreciation within your team.

I was talking to my client, Michelle, the other day who was raving about her new hire who worked offsite. She was telling me how amazing this employee was doing, that she was accomplishing tasks that Michelle didn't think she was going to be capable of doing for months, and how she was just blown away. I asked if this employee knew what Michelle thought of her work, or if she had heard this praise? Michelle responded that she thought so. My advice to Michelle was to make a point to speak her praise and appreciation. If this hadn't been done in a very specific way, then her employee probably did not know how Michelle felt. I advised her to send an email immediately stating exactly what she just shared with me, and to make it a practice to share these types of thoughts consistently with her team.

When I followed up with Michelle to ask how this had gone, I learned this simple email had made quite an impact on her new hire. She had never received an email which simply praised her for her work, and this encouragement was very much appreciated and needed. Setting up this dynamic of positive feedback under Michelle's leadership will begin to build trust in their relationship and prove to be very beneficial for them both.

Imagine if you received an email simply praising you for a job well done from your supervisor or manager? How would you feel? Would this boost your spirit and encourage you to work harder? I would bet the answer is yes. I would further theorize that receiving this type of communication regularly, building morale and trust, creates a willingness to say 'yes' when your supervisor needs to ask something of you beyond your normal duties such as taking on a bigger project or helping another department. Appreciating our team should be a practice we intentionally fold into our daily communication.

I remember clearly when a newer manager, Ray, came to me seeking advice. Ray had a horrible shift one night with an employee and she wanted advice on how to handle this situation and how she could avoid this in the future. She was clear on the fact that the interaction did not go well, and she knew she could have probably handled it better. Ray proceeded to walk me through the events of the night.

It was a hot and muggy summer evening in New York City. Ray was running low on some product and she asked an employee, Michael, to go and get the product for her from a sister-store. Michael was gone for what seemed a long time, and when he returned, there was a line of guests out the door. The team was completely behind and overwhelmed, being crushed with orders and people. Michael came in and threw the product on the shelf. He was drenched in sweat and looked very irritated.

Feeling overwhelmed and stressed herself, Ray's first words to him were: "What took you so long? Hurry up. We have a line out the door."

Michael then disappeared for a good half hour, which irritated Ray even more because it was obvious how much they needed his help. When Ray went to find Michael, he was sitting down with his head lowered, obviously dejected. Ray asked why he had not returned to help with the line of guests or why he was not starting on the dishes that were piling up. Michael then started yelling at her stating how unfair it was to be expected to do all the dishes himself when he just spent so much time running around getting the product. He was visibly upset and having a moment venting his frustrations. Ray took this outburst to be disrespectful and lashed back in kind. This continued until another employee came in asking Ray to help manage the line of guests.

During this conversation, Ray became a mirror for Michael. She mirrored his emotions/frustrations back at him. She allowed her emotions of the night to come into play and did not stop to consider his needs or how she could diffuse the situation by attending to his needs and help him feel appreciated. She did not listen but rather reacted. She had failed to be the effective leader she strived to be.

After listening to her story, I sat back, and I asked her some questions. How could that have gone differently? What was one thing you could have done differently to change the course of the interaction? What was he needing from you? She sat there for a bit and did not immediately reply. I allowed the silence, then asked, "If you were in Michael's position, what would you have wanted the moment you returned?" She answered, "Appreciation" and a smile came on her face as she realized her mistake. She then asked if I really thought things would have gone differently if she had just said "thank you"? Didn't he know she appreciated the errand but that things were obviously chaotic and stressful in the restaurant?

I asked her to look at the situation from his perspective, imagining she were him and I was her manager. I asked her to picture having to run out in the hot and humid NYC summer night, dealing with the subway and other irritated New Yorkers to get the necessary product from the other location. I then asked what she would have wanted to be said to her if she were in his position, walking in with the much-needed product. If upon walking in I said, "Oh my gosh, thank you so much! You're my lifesaver!" How would she feel at that moment? What if I went a step further and said something to the effect of, "Please get a quick, cold drink and take a few minutes, then I will help you crush the pile of dishes that are backed-up as soon as we're done with the line." How would that make her feel? Further, if I did ask for her help right away by saying, "Any chance you can help me out right now? You are my rock tonight!" What did she think her response would be? Ray just hung her head and said, "Yep, I missed that one." She said she was caught up in what *she* was experiencing and did not at all think about what *he* was experiencing. Ray said that if she had responded to Michael the way I just coached her, she knew without a doubt the evening would have been different.

The next day Ray was able to apologize to Michael and let him know how much she appreciated his help, both that night and during each shift they worked together. He walked away knowing he was valued, and they had a great relationship after the discussion. This is just one example of a conversation which impacted the work environment.

Smaller conversations happen throughout our shifts, throughout our days, and our work weeks. These often-overlooked little moments can swing the emotional pendulum of our team one way or the other dramatically. Great leaders are good at recognizing these moments to show appreciation and take advantage of them to ensure their people feel needed and valued.

Ray could have had an employee who felt appreciated and motivated, one that jumped back into the fray with her because he felt seen and valued. Instead, she had an employee who felt disgruntled even though he had done something which saved the day. He did not feel he was appreciated. This one simple act could have changed the entire course of the evening.

Chapter Three

Power Dynamics

Three types of power dynamics

I find it important to be aware of the power dynamics at play during conversations at work, as this will inform how you can have more successful conversations. What do I mean by this? There are typically multiple types of power dynamics you are going to deal with daily. The first type of dynamic would be with people who report directly to you. You have certain types of power over them. The second type of power dynamic is with people you consider peers or colleagues, as you are on the same level. The third type of power dynamic at play in your work environment is with your supervisor and those in higher positions. Being cognizant of these power dynamics is important when you are having conversations because this awareness will help you choose the right words to attain your end goal.

There are always power dynamics at play while at work. In any given interaction, you have the power, or the other person has some sort of power over you. Power over somebody else could mean you have the ability to affect their schedule, the projects they are going to get, and even their employment. Whether you choose to acknowledge it or not, this dynamic plays a part in every interaction and deserves some attention. Typically, your supervisor is not the only one who has power over you. Oftentimes your supervisor is coordinating with their peers when they pick who is going to be assigned to a project or who is going to get a promotion. Understanding these various dynamics and being curious about the needs of those at every level you are conversing with, will help you in meeting your end goals and have more productive conversations.

TYPE 1: SUBORDINATES

If you are the one who holds the power in the conversation, you have the responsibility to the person you are talking to. You do not have to tell others that you are in the power position. How many of us have worked for a leader who kept telling us that they were our boss? Does it build trust when somebody tells you they are your boss? No. Typically has the opposite effect, right? The more somebody tells me that they're my boss, the more I don't want to report to them.

It is how they lead which will inspire you to follow them or not. I often say a leader is only a leader if there are people following them. Otherwise, they're just a person out for a walk. You must have people who want to follow you in order to be a great leader.

The best leaders are the ones who look to serve others and are given authority because others want to follow them. To lead from a position of constantly trying to establish authority over others only makes you look weak and insecure, which again, doesn't inspire trust.

When you have all the power, you have an obligation to ensure that others feel safe and secure and not scared they're going to be punished for having an opinion. This is a big one. To be an effective leader, you need your employees to be comfortable disagreeing with you and voicing contrary perspectives to your ideas and plans. This doesn't naturally happen because your subordinates are aware of the power you have over them and might not want to do or say anything that could result in your use of power affecting them negatively. Therefore, you need to cultivate this dynamic of open dialogue without fear of retribution. This is not only healthy, but this will help you be successful. Oftentimes when I am thinking of starting an initiative or I am thinking of rolling something out, I will go to several different people and ask if I can pick their brains. Typically, I go to people I know will be reticent to the change or might be the hardest to win over. Why do I do this? Well, I truly want them to point out any gaps in my thinking before I finalize my plan, as it makes for a better plan. At the end of the day, if I have a blind spot I am not aware of, I'd much rather know about it before I present it to my boss or stakeholders rather than after. This provides me with critical feedback, and it makes it so that my project is much more successful.

This strategy also gets the person who would probably be my biggest defector on board from the jump because who doesn't want to be asked to share their opinion? Who doesn't want to be asked for their expertise? Everybody does. That's human nature. It's playing into the ego I know is present. Getting this feedback and pushback from the beginning allows me to build advocates for it out of the biggest possible opponents.

Asking for this type of feedback is critical; however, it might be hard for others to be honest with you at first. Some do not want to hurt your feelings, while others simply do not want to be punished by pointing out differences in opinion or your mistakes. To get the most helpful feedback possible, you must stress that you desire their dissenting opinions, and they won't be punished for giving it to you bluntly. Give them a safe space by expressing why their honesty at this moment is so important to you and allowing them to see that you crave the push back. This is what's needed oftentimes to convince your subordinates to open up.

It's helpful to explain to your team that there's a difference between speaking their mind when asked for it, versus, for instance, in the middle of a huge meeting and blindsiding you in front of the entire company. But, if you don't allow people to criticize you in private, then you might leave them little to no choice to do so publicly. This type of dialogue from our team is what we wish to avoid. It shows little trust and respect built.

Nobody wants to be on a team where they feel like they're not heard. The best way to ensure your team feels heard is to go to them first and ask their opinion and that any critical feedback or blind spots be discussed. These interactions go a long way to establish trust.

When a leader values feedback by asking for contribution and then gives the space to be honest in order to help a project be successful, their team is more apt to trust that leader in other areas as well. This safe place to exchange ideas is a major factor in creating a great team and company culture.

I went to a major Human Resources conference one year, and one of the seminars I attended was about performance management reviews. The presenter spoke about how the relationship between company and employee has changed dramatically since the Industrial Revolution, however the way we evaluate our employees hasn't. He spoke about how the relationship had previously been very transactional, meaning it was based on a strict contract. The employee did the contracted job then went home. This relationship has changed dramatically, as has the way we identify with our jobs and careers. Therefore, we want a job that engages us on many levels and aligns with our values and needs. He asked us to acknowledge that if our relationships have changed at work, we needed to rethink the way we managed performance as well. The example he gave us to consider is one I have often brought up with supervisors to get them to understand that to have a good relationship with their employees, they need to get their employees to buy-in.

The best leaders can inspire others because those following them buy-in to what they are promoting. The example he shared with us was this: Imagine that you had performance management reviews with your significant other, just like you do with your employees. Imagine it is the end of the year and you're sitting across from your partner and rating them on how they've performed over the last 6 months.

Maybe you're not happy with the way they've been loading the dishwasher recently, so you bring this up now and attach a score to it. You go through the entire scoring system until you get to the goal setting portion. Now you tell them, "I know you've been talking about wanting to lose weight, so I've decided that your goal should be to lose 10 pounds in the next 6 months." Just for a second, think about how your significant other would respond to this. You probably are laughing or shaking your head at this moment, knowing that this would elicit a strong reaction from your partner!

Instead, imagine sitting with your significant other and having a routine weekly or bi-weekly meeting to discuss how things are going. This is not a pressurized sit-down, because this is a part of your normal routine. You often sit and discuss things to ensure that you are on the same page and nothing goes too long without being addressed. Now imagine you start discussing goal setting and you ask your partner what goals they would like to commit to? They might offer up that they've been meaning to lose weight, so maybe they'll commit to losing 15 pounds. You may think this is out of reach and discuss reasonable expectations with them, explaining that you want to celebrate with them when they reach their goal, so maybe a more reasonable goal of 10 pounds would be good to start with. You might then talk about how you can support your partner in this endeavor, as you want them to accomplish this goal for their own happiness. I don't imagine this way of having the conversation would lead to the argument and/or break up that the previous one might have led to. Why? As you've probably already put together, it was because you asked them, rather than dictated to them. You included them in the process. This was also a normal kind of conversation rather than a pressurized review.

The first type of conversation placed you on opposite sides, with one feeling dictated to and without a voice. The second type of conversation places you both on the same side as a team with support built-in. These two choices of conversations are available at work as well. You can dictate to those you have power over, or you can have a consistent conversation, hearing them out, and seeking to support and guide. This is entirely up to you; however, you will get two very different outcomes. This second type of collaborative conversation pattern works well for today's workplace environment.

TYPE 2: PEERS

Too many times I've been asked to help manage relationships between peers that've gone bad. This dynamic is hard, as I find more times than not, both people want to ensure their power and authority are appreciated, which takes the focus off hearing the other person. Another factor at play is the way assumptions are active but not addressed.

One such situation was when two directors, Jeff and Kyra, got into a confrontation about a project that was being worked on between their two departments. A new system was being built and both needed to work on this project together to build the most effective system. Jeff took charge of the project, without really talking to Kyra. Jeff just assumed that he should take lead. Kyra, feeling sidelined and undervalued, decided to not attend any of the meetings she was invited to, as she did not feel needed.

When the project was just about ready to launch, Kyra decided to point out that there were massive errors needed to be addressed and that the system would not integrate with what was already in place. She suggested they needed to go back to the drawing board. This infuriated Jeff, as he felt that had Kyra attended the meetings, the issues could've been seen long before they got to the launch point. This ended up devolving into an ugly situation, which was when I was brought in.

How could this situation have been handled differently? Well, my first recommendation would be that there should have been a conversation at the outset of the project to decide who would lead, as well as who would be responsible for what. This conversation, if devoid of ego, could've set up the team to successfully work together. When strategy and boundaries are agreed to on the outset, then it is much easier to hold each other accountable when things go awry.

When Kyra chose not to attend the scheduled meetings, there should've been a discussion immediately. If she were told her feedback was essential, that she was needed and valued, and the project would not be as good if she weren't involved, I'm sure she would've had a far different attitude. As it was, when her lack of presence was noticed but not mentioned, this just contributed to her feeling unneeded and undervalued. Even though this wasn't the intention, it was the result of not asking why she wasn't at the meetings immediately.

Jeff, on the other hand, took Kyra's lack of participation as an afront and thought this was simply her way of being disrespectful. Assuming the lack of attendance was about himself caused Jeff to not be able to see how Kyra might be feeling and how her needs were not being addressed. There were several mediation sessions, and the project did get finished; however, the strain both continued to feel did not need to be present. Those offended feelings could've been avoided.

From an outside perspective, I'm sure most can see how easy this situation was to remedy at the moment, but I wonder how many times you yourself have been involved in this type of situation. I wonder how many times you have assumed feelings based on actions, not asking for clarification, but rather reacting based on perceived slights. Unfortunately, I know this is a common occurrence. Our egos are powerful, and the stories we tell ourselves are fraught with ego. Belief in these stories without clarification will end up hurting us in the long run. *Give the benefit of the doubt and ask for clarification.*

You might just find that the actions of the other person have nothing to do with you, but rather, attempts to try to meet their own needs. When we rely on our ego-filled stories to dictate our actions and reactions to others, we might miss a great opportunity to connect and to lead. Again, once assumptions are acted upon in response, hurt feelings are hard to undo after simmering for a long time. I challenge you to think about the situations in your life today where this may be at play.

Evaluate your own ego-driven narratives,
then give the benefit of the doubt and ask for
clarification out of curiosity.

This is the best way to communicate with peer relationships.

I've found myself in conversations where I get a sense that someone is expecting me to challenge their authority just by the way they're leading the meeting or discussion. At that moment, I can decide which path I want to take. Do I want to add to the combative environment, or do I want to diffuse it?

When I take the approach that they have expertise to aid in the discussion and when I express that I'm not there to challenge them but rather to support in any way I can, I've often been surprised by how quickly the energy of the room changes. I can sometimes see the change in them physically as well with a drop in their shoulders or a change in their facial expressions. This tells me they're more open to a dialogue.

So many times, I've then been able to work well with that person going forward, because I valued what they brought to the table, and wasn't there to challenge them or their authority. Funny enough, this typically has only aided to my power or authority, as the soft skills I was able to employ are often so much more powerful than the hard bluster that I had been presented with.

TYPE 3: SUPERIORS

So many of us have been fortunate to work with some amazing leaders and supervisors who have embodied the qualities discussed so far. Those who have made sure we feel seen, heard and appreciated. We've also, most likely, all worked for people who did not embody these qualities and we might have taken that very personally. When I am working for somebody who seems to have a chip on their shoulder, it usually has to do with their own insecurities rather than major flaws on my end. Even though your superiors have a power dynamic over you which might have some effect on you such as your job duties, etc., do not give over your power of self-worth so easily.

Again, being aware of the energy from the supervisor as well as giving the benefit of the doubt is what I fall back on. I try to tap into what the person's fears, concerns, or needs are. If I'm completely lost on this, I might go so far as to ask them. This is as easy as "What are some of your fears or concerns surrounding this?" This way I know exactly what I need to consider going forward when looking to pitch an idea or project. Oftentimes, this saves me a lot of work in the long run.

Voicing that the superior will make the final decision is an example of a great communication tool in a common interaction. A superior can feel I might make a move or decision without them, which could be a fear. I let them know I value their position and will keep them in the loop. I convey that I won't make any final decisions but will let them make the final call. I also change my word choice to reflect this thought process when presenting my ideas. I don't "tell" them what we should do, I "recommend", or "suggest."

I'm intentional with our communication and am consistently the first to catch them up to speed. By doing this, they never have to ask me as I'm beating them to it with the information they need. I'm anticipating their questions and filter my talking points to always cover what their fears are first. This allows them to understand that I'm not there to challenge them or their position, but rather I'm there to assist and support. Typically, this leads to more autonomy given to me, as the relationship is built with the trust that I know their concerns and will strive to alleviate them.

CHAPTER FOUR

PREPARATION

UNEXPECTED CONVERSATIONS THAT ARE DIFFICULT

Often, there will be no warning that you are entering into a difficult conversation and you won't be able to prepare. I once had an entire situation unravel from the very innocent question: "How are you today?"

One afternoon, I received a call from a manager stating she didn't know what to do with an employee as she found him to be very disrespectful. I inquired for further information and was told that the manager, Sonja, had greeted an employee, Jared, that day by asking, "How are you doing today?" Jared answered, "Fine, until I saw I was working with you." When I asked what Sonja replied, she stated that she said nothing back. I would love to say I was shocked by her lack of curiosity. However, by then I was not surprised by others' desire to avoid these moments of tension. Sometimes people are just caught off guard and not prepared to enter into a difficult conversation.

I told Sonja this was a great opportunity to ask a question out of curiosity. The question could've been simply, "Oh no, why is that?" Which would've allowed Jared to reveal what the issue was. I headed over to that restaurant and Sonja invited Jared to join us for a conversation. When I asked this simple question, the why, we uncovered that Jared had heard Sonja didn't like him and believed that to be true based on the fact that Sonja constantly gave what Jared thought to be the hardest job in the restaurant, the grill station.

Sonja was flabbergasted to hear this, as she thought Jared was a very hard worker and put him on the grill because she trusted him more than anyone else on this station. Sonja went on to praise Jared, which was sadly surprising for him to hear.

He lit up hearing this praise and voiced that he agreed it took skill to work this station well. Jared started to see his positioning as more of an accomplishment rather than the punishment he originally had viewed it to be.

We ended the conversation with the agreement that going forward, should Jared hear anything or think there were issues, he'd bring them up immediately to Sonja in a way that was simply seeking information. Sonja agreed to do a better job explaining why she assigned stations the way she did and to start complimenting her team much more at the moment she noticed their hard work. At the end of the day, it was a great conversation – but one that shouldn't have been initiated by so much frustration.

Difficult conversations pop up when we least expect it and will often catch us off guard. You can prepare for these unexpected conversations by practicing habits like awareness of others' reactions to you, asking questions in the moment from a place of curiosity, and having the intention to ensure that all feel seen, heard and appreciated. These daily practices will aid you greatly in preparing for those unexpected issues and surprising conversations.

PREPARING FOR HARD CONVERSATIONS

Take the time to prepare for conversations you know will be uncomfortable or downright difficult. We tend to think preparation might make the conversation mechanical but when you prepare correctly, the conversation will go much smoother and your team will feel supported and cared for. The following are the preparation habits I've established over my years as a leader that I know will be invaluable to you as well.

FALSE NARRATIVES

It's important to understand that we tell ourselves false narratives every day. You may notice during a meeting that someone seems to refuse to look at you. You may find yourself saying "hi" to someone, and they don't answer you. In these moments, oftentimes, we create stories around the why, which usually has everything to do with us in our minds but may not have any basis in reality. "They must be mad at me because they didn't look at me at all," you might think. "They must hate working with me because they didn't say 'hi'," you could reason. In our minds, these slights are intentional and have everything to do with us, however, in reality, this is often just not the case.

The person who did not look at you might have just caught a mistake they made and were mortified. The person that did not reply to your 'hi' may have not heard you because they were caught up in their own thoughts. The reality is, we all have so many things going on, and often these perceived slights have nothing to do with what we assume they do.

When preparing to enter into any difficult conversation, start by asking yourself, what am I assuming and what do I know for sure?

We are hardly ever the center of anybody else's story, and the assumptions we make may lead us down a path that will harm our working relationships.

When others are having a bad day, it is very rarely because of us and more likely because of things that have happened in their own lives throughout their day. The difficult part is recognizing reality. This means we must check our ego. Let go of the impulse that "it" must be about me and enter into the space of curiosity.

What could be going on in their lives that you do not know about that could be influencing their attitude, words, or performance while at work?

GOALS AND INTENTIONS

It's important to fully understand what your goals are prior to having a difficult conversation. It's also helpful to state the goals beforehand. For example, maybe you noticed an employee has been coming in late, and you know you need to address this. By only telling them that you would like to speak with them might create anxiety within them. By not knowing the goals of the conversation, they're left to wonder if they are in trouble or even getting fired. They might come into the conversation already on the defense emotionally.

> *Stating your goals of the conversation beforehand*
> *will allow others time to process and come to the*
> *conversation more openly and engagingly,*
> *rather than starting with a defensive posture.*

With the example of an employee being late, you could state that you would like to talk to them about the fact they've been coming in late and you would like to find a solution for this. Stating why you would like to speak with them as well as the goal of the conversation will allow them to see that you want to work with them and find a solution; in other words, you are a support and want to help.

Stating the reasons and goals upfront not only allows all involved to understand what the conversation is about but also gives you something to circle back to should the conversation go off course. This can create a much calmer dialogue and allow each participant to be fully present with their defenses down.

Questions to ask yourself before the conversation to help organize what your goals are:

- What is the issue?

- What is this conversation about?

- What is the goal of the conversation?

- What is the ideal outcome?

GATHER FACTS

It's important to know your facts and not base a conversation on assumptions or hyperbole in order to have a successful dialogue.

An example of a conversation starting with hyperbole is if you say, "You're always late," when the fact might be this person was late three times over the past three weeks. *Stating facts, not hyperbole, helps facilitate getting to the root cause and avoids the conversation devolving into an argument.*

Fact: when you use the words 'always' or 'never', you're setting yourself up for a bad conversation. Let's be honest, very rarely does something always or never happen. Typically, it's only a handful of times or that you're noticing a pattern. Patterns are typically what we're addressing. Learn specific words to describe the behavior.

An example would be, "I would like to talk about the pattern of lateness I've been noticing." Using specific behavior words is a much more honest way to start the conversation and one that is rooted in fact and can be proven. "I can pull up your clock-in times to show that you have been late three out of the past five shifts," is another example of using specific behavior verbiage. You want the dialogue to be around why this is happening and possible solutions, rather than arguing about what's taken place already. Therefore, you want to be able to state the facts and move on to the whys and solutions.

Gather all proof of the facts you would like to present. For example, if the conversation is about an employee not wearing the correct uniform, don't waste time arguing about that fact, but have camera images (if available) prepared and ready to be shown to the employee. This will enable you to talk about the solutions very early in the conversation. Gathering your facts with any proof beforehand sets the stage for a much shorter and productive conversation than if you were to not have the facts and proof present. This also avoids hurt feelings which often come with a defensive debate over facts.

Taking the time to prepare by setting your goals and intentions, deciding on a private space, and gathering all your facts and any proof available as well as how you are going to state those facts will allow you to spend the allotted time of the meeting focusing on understanding the situation better and finding a solution, rather than debating the problem stated.

This will also ensure a much smoother conversation that has less chance of being hijacked by interruptions or digressions into other topics

THE ENVIRONMENT

If your workplace is a restaurant, the environment is going to most likely be a little crazy. Operations are always happening, so it's important to find a space that's quiet, or as quiet as possible. Finding a private or semi-private place, away from others who may overhear the conversation, helps your team member feel safe to share. Sitting with your back to the action will allow you to focus on who you are talking to, rather than get distracted by what is going on.

If you're in an office environment, scheduling time in the conference room or finding a space you two can talk in a private area is preferred. This should be somewhere your team member doesn't feel like all eyes are on them.

When thinking through the setting to have a difficult conversation, it is helpful to ask yourself how you'd like to be treated if the roles were reversed. I once had a colleague who shared that a previous organization she worked for had a glass-enclosed conference room in the middle of the office. When she had a meeting in this room, she felt like the eyes of the entire office were on her. While no one could hear the conversation, she felt on display for all. This didn't elicit a safe and comfortable feeling.

The lesson is, be mindful when you're seeking a place to have a difficult conversation. Be respectful of the other person and think through how they might feel in the physical space you choose. Their feelings of safety may impact the conversation.

Limiting interruptions is also important to help others feel valued. Have you ever been in the middle of a conversation with a supervisor, maybe a scheduled performance review, or getting critical feedback on a project, and their phone went off and they chose to answer? How did you feel? Did you feel important and valued? Or did you feel second best? Nobody wants to feel second best, so you must honor those you meet with by making sure that, if at all possible, you limit interruptions during a conversation. If you should get interrupted with something beyond your control, acknowledge that it isn't ideal and let them know it's not a reflection of how you value them. Life happens. Things happen which may demand your attention at the moment. Apologize if this happens. Explain the situation, and acknowledge that it's not acceptable, however, it is reality.

Either ask for the time you need to deal with a situation or to reschedule if needed. If you do ask for time, respect the time you state and honor that commitment by not keeping them waiting beyond what you agreed to.

Again, urgent situations beyond our control happen sometimes. But if interruptions are a common occurrence, then this may have to do with other issues you should investigate and deal with. These issues might be problems in the overall communication strategy and structure of the organization. If your department is always operating in fire-fighting mode, meaning it's the norm to fly from one emergency to the next, then there are deeper issues to sort out. Honoring commitments is what builds trust. You can have the best notes, intentions, and preparation for the conversation, however, if you consistently blow off commitments because of distractions or emergencies, the actions that you take will have much more of an impact than the words you use or preparation you put in.

CHECK YOUR EGO

It is difficult to create a space for a conversation where your team feels safe and cared for if we are coming from a place of ego first. You will know if your ego is involved if you are personally offended by their lack of performance. If you see a team member's lateness as a personal affront to you, then your ego is active, and the conversation will not be as fruitful. To create a safe space for your team, we must leave our ego out of it and realize the majority of the issues we deal with have nothing to do with us.

No, your employee isn't coming in late because she wants to disrespect you. Their tardiness has nothing to do with you at all. By putting aside the ego and getting curious, your entire demeanor will change and you will be showing that you are here for your team and you want them to feel safe in coming to you with issues so you can find the best solution for all. When you lead with your ego, your demeanor and words will most likely create more strife and the best solution will not be found.

I remember when I became a General Manager for the first time. I was a young female in a very male-dominated industry. My ego shield was fully up, and I was ready for any incoming slights.

I had to learn the hard way that not everything is about me. Instead of assuming the reason one of the cooks didn't follow my instructions was because I was just a 'young girl', maybe, just maybe, the refusal to follow directions had more to do with him than me! When I entered the conversation thinking it was because of my age or my gender, the conversation was confrontational. When I entered into a conversation with curiosity and wanting to understand, I was able to have many more fruitful conversations which led to both parties giving the benefit of the doubt in the moment, and future interactions as well.

*By making sure your ego is in check and that
you are creating a safe space for your employees,
you indicate that you are here to support them to ensure
success for all.*

Taking the time to prepare by checking your assumptions and ego, setting your intentions, gathering all your facts and proof, and intentionally deciding on an environment conducive to a sensitive conversation will set you up for success.

CHAPTER FIVE

THE CONVERSATION

WHAT IS A DIFFICULT CONVERSATION?

Any conversation where there might be contrasting viewpoints can be difficult. A conversation in which at least one person is uncomfortable or feels the need to defend themselves can be difficult. Conversations which point out flaws or mistakes made can be very difficult. If you are a leader, you will *need* to have these types of conversations. If you are a good leader, you won't avoid them but will develop the skills to be able to enter into them with confidence, kindness, and tact.

COMPONENTS OF A CONVERSATION

Stating goals is laying the foundation for the conversation. Often, when we are having conversations, we can tend to go on different tangents.

You might be talking about one issue, but then maybe because the employee is defensive and wants to deflect, they bring up a whole host of issues they have been holding onto and are dissatisfied with. While each of their feelings and points may be valid, without a foundation to hold onto, you may end up going down rabbit holes. When you have the goal at hand, you can validate their feelings, however, continue to come back to the goal to keep the conversation on track.

You've already prepared for the conversation by telling your employee before meeting why you're wanting to speak with them and the goal of the meeting. Start the conversation by reiterating the goal(s) of the meeting so you can both keep it as the focus.

Simon Sinek, motivational speaker and author of such books as *The Infinite Game* and *Leaders Eat Last*, has outlined a great way to think about the components of the conversation that is quite helpful. He advises thinking about having difficult conversations at work by utilizing the acronym **F.B.I.**[7]

F.B.I.

F is to state how you feel. This is important because, often-times, we don't state how we feel, but instead, we state what we think we know about the other person. So instead of saying, "I feel frustrated that you've repeatedly come to work late," we might say something like, "You obviously don't care about this job because you've come in late every day." We don't have any idea if they care about the job or not. We have stated what we *think* they feel, rather than what we *know*. We know what *our* feelings are and should state those. If we state what we think about them and not what we know about us, it might lead to a debate over whether they care about their job or not. This isn't what you intended to discuss. Your issue was their tardiness. By stating how you feel, you can keep the issue on their tardiness, and start to have a meaningful conversation. Therefore, simply state how you feel because this is what you know. The rest you should get curious

---

[7] https://simonsinek.com/commit/feedback-and-recognition/

about. We can be wrong if we assume other people's intentions or feelings, but we cannot be wrong about our own feelings.

B is for what the Behavior is. Keeping to the same example of tardiness, you could state, "You've come in at least twenty minutes late four out of your last five shifts." This is not a point that can be debated but can be backed by actual data. This is where your preparation of gathering facts comes in useful. By stating factual behavior, we avoid shaming or demeaning, but rather keep to an account of the events. Sometimes employees don't realize the actual data of their behavior and it's eye-opening to see the plain facts of what their behavior is without emotion involved.

I is for Impact. State what the impact of their behavior is. This could sound like, "By coming in late, you impact the entire team as they have to do your job as well as their own. I don't want to, however, if this behavior continues, I may need to look to schedule someone else." Many aren't aware of how their behavior might negatively affect their team. When pointed out, I often find that people are surprised by how they affect others, and feel quite bad about it, as it's not their intention. I've never spoken to anyone who purposely wanted to do a bad job while at work. Most want to be successful but don't understand how they might be their own biggest obstacle to success.

List the impact of their actions and then stop speaking for a moment. This is where most get uncomfortable and just keep talking, which either distracts from your main point or worse yet, takes the conversations completely off-topic. It's important to stop and, if needed, count to 10 (or 20!) in silence to let the other person explain their behavior or admit there is an issue. I recognize that sitting in silence is very uncomfortable at first, and many will wish to fill this space of silence. I challenge you to get comfortable with uncomfortable silence. The tendency is to want to fill the silence by continuing to state our points or say how we feel and drone on and on. *The silence is important in conversations.* It's okay to wait for a beat and let them process what they have heard. After giving them a moment and being patient, they might start bringing up off-topic points. Simply come back to stating how you feel, their behavior, and the impact it has had. Then you can explain that you want to understand why this is an issue and you want to help find a possible solution that meets everyone's needs.

To summarize the components of **FBI**:

F: state how you *Feel*

B: state what the *Behavior* is

I: state what the *Impact* of the behavior is

These are the main components of the conversation.

The foundation is your intention of every conversation and the goals are specific for each conversation. My intention is to leave the other person feeling seen, heard, and appreciated. Your goals are the specific outcomes you would like to see achieved. Once you have your goals set, have determined how you feel, what the specific behavior is, and how the behavior has made an impact, you have the talking points of a great conversation.

AVOIDING TANGENTS

Tangents are going to happen. People are going to get defensive and try to deflect. Understand this is normal, expect it, and commit to coming back to the goal of the conversation. This will help you navigate the tangents.

Step one is to not take the bait. Remember what was learned earlier about mirroring. Do not mirror their energy and let your ego get involved. I would advise you to not shut down their points or start defending yourself, but rather ask them to pause on the discussion point until you can fully address the original intent of the conversation.

Be humble and don't let your ego overtake the conversation. This will aid in your success as you navigate through the conversation. This might sound like "I'm sure that you might be right, and I know there are things that I could do better. I'm interested in hearing about them, but we'll have to circle back to those points after resolving the issue at hand." Or "We can certainly address each of your points next, however right now I'd like to focus on the pattern of lateness and what we can do about it going forward." These statements acknowledge their frustrations and lets them know you are open to hearing about them and that you realize you have flaws. This also makes it clear that you won't be deterred from addressing what you need to address.

REMEMBER TO LISTEN

With your point handy and your nerves in overdrive, you may be inclined to rush through your points to get the conversation done. Remember, that is not the goal. The goal is to better understand the issues at play and find a solution which works for all. *To do this, you must listen. Not wait to talk. Not listen to speak. But listen to understand.* Without doing this, you won't find the best long-term solution, and you'll miss what the root cause of the issue is.

How many times have you been in a conversation with somebody and they ask you questions but don't even wait for answers? Don't you hate that? In a difficult conversation, this typically takes place because the person leading the conversation is nervous. Leaders typically don't want to be seen as not in control and so they talk a lot and fill all the space. Sometimes they simply want to cross this conversation off their to-do list, and so they're rushing to "get it over with." This is a mistake, as the silence is really where the golden nuggets are. As I stated previously, I suggest you start getting comfortable with silence. Be comfortable with asking a question and sitting there for a minute or two until that person comes back with an answer. If they look at you to save them, let them know you will give them time to think of their answer. Know that it will be uncomfortable and start being okay with that.

Sometimes, in these moments of silence, one minute can feel like fifteen minutes. It's just a minute, and we can all afford a minute to sit while somebody ponders a question. By doing this, not only will you allow them to answer your question with a thoughtful response, possibly getting to the root cause, but you're also showing them with your actions that they're worth your time. You're saying to them, "You are worth me sitting with you while you contemplate the question I have asked" which can be huge. Silence can be good. Sometimes it can bring up some deeper understanding you never thought possible.

I urge you to get comfortable with silence and to remind yourself in those moments that silence could be very helpful in allowing us to connect with the person we are talking to.

BE CURIOUS TO FIND OUT THE WHY

If you aren't curious, you will continue to put a band-aid on a broken bone. What do I mean by that? Imagine the root cause of an issue is the broken bone. Simply having a transactional conversations where you tell the employee what they're doing wrong repeatedly and let them know what the penalty is, is much like putting a band-aid on the issue. Having a deeper transformational conversation where you get curious and seek out the root cause to identify solutions tailored to the issue is setting the bone.

One is a temporary fix, the other is a more permanent fix. Thinking about the example of the conversation with an employee about being late, you could just tell this employee that if they continue to be late, they'll be written up. This is the penalty for being late. End of discussion. This kind of conversation is a band-aid. You haven't addressed what the root cause is, and so often, the issue will continue to persist because you haven't addressed the why.

If, instead of just letting the employee know about the policy and penalty for coming late, you got curious as to why they were coming in late, you have more of a chance to find out the root cause and come up with a solution agreeable to all which would have long-lasting results. There was a reason you hired this person. You have invested in them through orientation, training, and coaching. So why throw that all away? When you get curious, you can identify what might not have been obvious, which will lead to a better solution and in turn, could help reset this employee to be successful in the long run.

Let's say you have an employee, Shannon, who you hired because she had amazing experience, an awesome personality, and has shown herself to be a very hard worker. Lately, she's been coming in about 30 minutes late for her 7 A.M. shift. When you get curious as to the why, you find out that Shannon isn't late for a lack of trying, but rather, because the bus route she needs to take each day is extremely close to the time she needs to send her children off for school. If everything in the morning went perfectly, Shannon would arrive on time for work at exactly 7 A.M.

Unfortunately, nothing goes perfectly every day. Between kids running late, busses being off schedule, and just the random commuter inconveniences we expect, it's not surprising to see why Shannon has been late. Upon getting curious, you find out that if you swapped out a shift with another employee so Shannon was scheduled for 8 A.M. rather than 7 A.M., this would make a world of difference for her. Now, you might be thinking, why didn't Shannon ask for this schedule change herself? Well, how many times have you needed something from your supervisor or boss, and have been scared to ask for it? How many times have you feared that if you did not just do as you were told, you might be out of a job? Or have you ever tried to make do so you would not look weak or incompetent? This happens more than we care to admit. The reason you have been put in a position of leadership is to come up with creative solutions. You can't do this if you don't understand the full issue at hand.

We must be open to the conversation going in a direction we might not anticipate. Being curious means we might not know the answer, but are open to where the conversation may take us. Let's go back to the story of David who started dropping the ball and his overall performance was lacking. He used to be high energy, but lately, the energy level had drastically lowered. Sarah, his manager, had a purely transactional conversation about specific mistakes on his projects. The conversation will probably not result in long-lasting change. What if Sarah had gotten curious instead and asked David about why his demeanor had changed? She might've learned that his parent or family member was dealing with a serious health problem, and this caused him to be stressed as well as taken a lot of his free time. Sarah probably would be caught off-guard and not expect such an answer. But she could stay present and fully engaged. Not only would this be an opportunity to connect on a human level, but this would have most likely led to brainstorming for solutions.

SHOW EMPATHY FOR EMPLOYEE'S FEELINGS

Showing empathy and having a human to human moment, is what is needed from leaders in conversations like these. Asking how we can support is the helpful next step. Sometimes there is nothing we can do, however knowing that you're in their corner and just offering support may be exactly what the employee needs from us. Other times, there may be concrete ways in which you can help.

This is where you can get creative as a leader. Maybe a schedule change is needed. Maybe some time off to deal with this issue would be most helpful. Maybe just the emotional support you offer is what they need to be their best selves at work right now. But you must be open to diving deeper in conversations, and sometimes that simply means showing a little empathy. Be courageous, have the conversation, and lead with your intentions to help your team be their best.

Empathy is defined as the action of understanding, being aware of, being sensitive to, and vicariously experiencing the feelings, thoughts, and experiences of another of either the past or present without having the feelings, thoughts, and experience fully communicated in an objectively explicit manner.[8] The fact that you do not agree with another person doesn't mean their feelings are wrong or any less valid. The ideal is to see things through their eyes. Brené Brown explains that "To empathize with someone's experience you must be willing to believe them as they see it, and not how you imagine their experience to be.[9]" I find during a stressful or difficult conversation, we can get very stuck in how we perceive the situation.

---

[8] https://www.merriam-webster.com/dictionary/empathy
[9] "The Social Dilemma" on Netflix

When we can instead approach a conversation with empathy, we keep an open perspective, rather than thinking from our perspective only. We can then communicate that the others' feelings are valid before speaking to how we might be able to rectify the issue.

KITCHEN SINK CONVERSATIONS

Kitchen sink conversations don't make people feel safe and cared for. What do I mean by kitchen sink conversations? A kitchen sink conversation is when you take a moment in a discussion to voice your frustrations about everything possible (including the kitchen sink) rather than sticking to one issue or a pattern. An example of a Kitchen Sink Conversation would be if you're talking about one particular issue, perhaps a spreadsheet that was wrong with your supervisor, and they decide to bring up unresolved issues they've had with you, unbeknownst to you, for the past six weeks. They might bring up the fact that they've noticed you've been coming in later or that you have started wearing jeans and not dress slacks. Oftentimes they will include what you view as petty issues that they seem to have been holding onto for a while. The issues they are bringing up catch you off-guard, as they've never mentioned anything about it until this moment. Now, the conversation isn't just about a mistake on a spreadsheet but has diverted to include an entire host of issues. You are probably pretty taken aback, as you didn't have any clue to their dissatisfactions. You might even start thinking about all the times your supervisor has smiled at you or complimented you in recent weeks, wondering if those interactions were genuine.

Think about how this type of interaction would make you feel. Would you feel safe? Would this kind of conversation build trust with your supervisor? My guess is the answers are "no." You might wonder if there are other issues held back that might come up later? Resentment might start to build if you thought they were happy with you and now question that belief.

Trust can be shattered by these types of conversations. If you hold issues in and eventually throw the kitchen sink into your conversations, your team will begin to realize they cannot trust you. It is imperative to not avoid difficult conversations but instead be honest when issues arise. When your team knows you will bring up issues promptly and not throw issues of the past into conversations, they know they can always trust what you say. They know you will be honest and transparent with them, which makes them feel safe and cared for.

CHAPTER SIX

WORDS MATTER

THREE QUESTIONS

When I remind myself of what my intentions are, then I'm more apt to become curious as to how the other person is viewing the situation and what their perception or experience is. Seeking to understand and find solutions is what I try to hold as my intent during any conversation, regardless of the topic.

This gives me a goal at the outset that is clear, allowing me to shape the conversation through this lens. Anytime I am speaking, whether it is in a group or a one-on-one conversation, I try to ask myself three questions before opening my mouth.

They are:

1. Is it true?

2. Is it kind?

3. Is it necessary?

Oftentimes, a statement or phrase is true but might not be kind. Sometimes it is both true and kind, however, not necessary. When we try to limit what we say to ensure all three of these boxes are ticked, then we're more apt to not regret what we say.

Asking myself: "Is it true?" allows me to question the facts. Using the example of having a conversation about an employee being late, if we were to say to them, "You are always late," this is most likely not a true statement. When we look at the facts, we might uncover they've been late three out of the last five shifts. While this may not be acceptable, it's not in fact "always." By simply stating facts and not being hyperbolic, we can deal with the real issue, and not get caught up on hyperbole.

Asking myself: "Is it kind?" will allow me to analyze if I'm being snarky or stating something in a way that will automatically make the other person defensive. If I make the person or group I am speaking with defensive right away, they are less apt to hear what I'm trying to say. They may then be less inclined to collaborate on finding solutions or rally to my cause in any way. Ensuring that I am being kind doesn't mean sugarcoating something, however, it simply means choosing words infused with goodwill.

The question of: "Is it necessary?" is a bit harder, but so very important. How many times have you witnessed interactions escalate because both parties seem to need the last word? Or how many times have you been in a conversation that has gone sideways because the person just had to add in their thoughts or opinions that weren't needed, but seemed to give them a chance to hear their own voice? Stating only what is necessary is a skill which must be practiced, however once learned, can set you apart and will make your words so much more valuable when you do speak. The person who speaks with authority and fewer words than the rest is typically the one that is listened to the most, and whose opinion is sought out.

Being intentional with your words means you will regret saying things a lot less and will allow your message to come across clearly and with authority. These three questions are on a plaque on my desk, and they are my go-to in any conversation.

THE POWER OF WE

When I'm having a conversation, difficult or not, I try not to phrase anything with a 'me versus them' approach. I want to ensure the person I am talking to knows that I'm on their team and that we have a common goal we are working towards together.

To do this, I make sure my words are echoing this sentiment. I use words like "we" when talking through options. Using "we" implies that the work is shared, the end goal is shared, and that the team is behind each member.

Read each of these sentences both ways:

"I think you can do a better job on this presentation" **vs** "I think we can do a better job on this presentation."

"I think you could've done a better job of preparing for yesterday's call" **vs** "I think we could've done a better job of preparing for yesterday's call."

Do you feel the difference by just replacing the word "you" with "we"? Usually, when I use the "you" sentences, it brings up people's defenses. When I use "we" it might sting a bit but coupled with a specific way you think it could be better, the team member will most likely be less defensive and more inclined to hear what you are saying and consider the feedback. How our words land and make others feel is what we need to be mindful of when we have conversations that might be difficult.

BALANCE THE FEEDBACK

We talked previously about giving positive feedback, and I think it is especially important to remember when you're giving critical feedback as well. If you're working with somebody and you didn't like how they put together, say, a spreadsheet, start with what you liked about it and be specific before stating any critiques. This might sound like, "Hey, I really liked how you laid out the spreadsheet and the colors you used. I thought it was great to see the different colors because it allowed me to see the difference in data points. That being said, I do think we need to fill in more of this data, so people understand what we're trying to point out." This will help the person get clear about what you do not want to be changed, and then hear what changes you do want. This also helps with diffusing defensiveness and increases the ability of our team to hear the critical feedback we are giving.

Often, our supervisors and managers only focus on the changes they want to see made. So, if I'm working on a project and my supervisor only tells me what they don't like about it, I may end up changing what they actually do like about the project without knowing it. This happened to me early in my career. I was working on a big project that would impact everyone in the company. When I met with my supervisor, he had a long list of changes to be made. He did not share with me what he liked at all, leaving me with the indication that he didn't like anything. He asked me to "go back to the drawing board", so that's exactly what I did. I worked nights and weekends completely redoing the entire project. When I presented it to him again, he was horrified to see many of the features he had loved were gone. I felt completely dejected to find out I had spent hours redoing things he had liked. Do not do this to your team. They'll feel crushed and defeated, just as I did.

Be clear when you give feedback, whether in the moment or during a more formal sit down. When you're clear about what you like and what you want to see changed or improved, your team will feel valued for what they've contributed and will be clear on what you would like to see going forward.

THOUGHTS ON THE OREO COOKIE APPROACH TO FEEDBACK

Many people like to give feedback with the Oreo cookie approach. This approach is where you give positive feedback, followed by critical feedback, and end with positive feedback. Some think this softens the blow of the critical feedback. In my experience, I have seen this only confuse the person who is receiving the feedback.

Often, this is because the person giving the feedback is so nervous they will upset the other person, that they completely overdo the positive feedback, and only skim over the critical portion. By starting and ending with positive comments, it's easy to forget or disregard the more critical part of the conversation.

The result is typically that the person receiving feedback walks away thinking only of the positive and does not hear the critical piece. I am a fan of positive feedback first followed by critical feedback. With this technique, they are not defensive when they hear the critical, however, they walk away clearly understanding what needs to change going forward.

STAY WITH YOUR GOALS AND INTENTIONS FOR THE CONVERSATION

We talked about how a conversation can venture off the path at various times, either when the other person deflects, decides to "kitchen sink" the conversation, or when there's an off-road to a back and forth about one of the points you may have brought up.

Prepare for these times, practice for them, and be ready. For me, this includes reminding myself constantly before the conversation about what my goals and intentions are. I have even gone so far as to write them down on a sticky note and put it on my notebook I take with me into a meeting.

Your intention is what's going to be the foundation for the conversation. You always need to remember how you want to impact your team member. Using the intention as a foundation, the goals of the conversation are the touchpoints that you can come back to should things start to spiral. Sometimes even verbalizing that you have seemed to go off-course and you would like to get back to the goals for the conversation will help reset the energy.

Make notes of the different points brought up. Maybe they lashed out and said you were horrible at scheduling; maybe they stated that you've been playing favorites because somebody else has also not been doing a great job and you haven't called them out. Make notes to follow up on their comments, however, continue to come back to your goals so you can get the conversation you want. Don't negate these points or ignore them. Let them know these are topics that you'd like to circle back to, but that you need to focus the time you have on the main reason you are speaking to them. Remind them that you can come back to the crucial issues they have brought up.

CHAPTER SEVEN

AWARENESS AND EMOTIONAL INTELLIGENCE

Words you choose to use are extremely important. However, feelings and body language in communication cannot be ignored.

PHYSICAL RESPONSES

What is the point of a conversation if our audience does not get our message? Our audience is not going to get our message if they are on the defense. With some people, the physical reaction to becoming defensive is the same as becoming angry. The physical response of anger will work against your end goal.

When triggered by anger or becoming defensive, elevated cortisol levels will cause the loss of neurons in the front of the brain or the prefrontal cortex.[10]

This elevated cortisol level suppresses activity in this part of the brain where you make good decisions and plan for the future. This release of cortisol will then kill neurons in the hippocampus or disrupt new ones from being created. This then weakens the short-term memory and prevents new memories from being properly formed. *And all of this can happen in half a second.*

How many times have you been in an argument and forgot to say something crucial? We have all said things in heated conver-

---

[10] https://www.nicabm.com/how-anger-affects-the-brain-and-body-infographic/

sations that we didn't mean but which had long term consequences. When we're angry, we don't think through the impact of our statements. This is a very real issue when we get angry because our bodies physically react to the anger and create the opposite criteria for a collaborative solution-oriented conversation.

Once we've triggered somebody to defensiveness or anger, it's very hard to stop the physical response which follows. The intention should be to not trigger someone at all, hoping to not have a full release of cortisol so that they can hear you fully and process what you are saying. By utilizing the information given in this book, you can decrease the chance of someone getting angry or defensive during a difficult conversation.

What do we do if we trigger a negative reaction in someone during a conversation? How do we undo this? Well, since time travel has not yet been mastered, I would suggest apologizing. Admitting that you did not phrase something correctly is key. Giving space and allowing some silence is also sometimes helpful. I have even gone so far as to ask the other person to take three or four deep breaths with me to reset. This allows the cortisol levels to drop, and clearly shows that I take responsibility for getting us to this stage. Admitting error and resetting the emotions of the moment may allow you to get back on track. If not, you may want to pause the conversation and take it up again later in the day or the next to allow for both parties to calm down. Nothing good will come of trying to jam through a conversation when emotions are too high.

TONE

Tone is just as important as word choice. Think about any sentence and think about the different tones that could be used to change the meaning. "I didn't know you would be here," can be said in different ways. "I didn't know *you* would be here," versus "I didn't know you would be *here.*" These two sentences read the same on paper but take on very different meanings when said with different tones. The first one could be said with the "you" emphasized and taken in a snide way. The second one, with the emphasis on "here" could indicate that it is a good surprise.

Tone is key, and unfortunately, a simple change in tone is sometimes all that needs to take place for a person to feel offended. Paying attention to your tone and inquiring when the other person's tone strikes you as offensive, is helpful when building great professional relationships.

TECHNOLOGY

Unfortunately, tone is hard to nail down in an email or text message. "How would you read this?" is one of the questions I get asked the most. Often, people assume a certain tone is implied in an email. Sometimes, the sender of the email has not indicated very well what their intentions are or how the reader should be taking things, leaving the reader to come to their own assumptions.

I find the people who are great communicators through email do not leave this up to the reader. They clearly state the intention of the email and add in communication points that lets the reader know their tone. Whether you're being playful or serious, you must be clear, so the reader does not assume the worst.

I strive to clearly state why I'm writing, what my intention is, and often also clearly state what I'm not trying to do. This could look like, "I'm writing to gain clarification, as I'm a bit confused. I'm not seeking to argue your point or in any way saying you are wrong, however, need some help understanding more fully." I realize my position of power and understand that without some clarity, my emails could read as cold and critical to someone who does not work with me daily. I can be sarcastic and I'm direct. Knowing this about myself, coupled with my position, means I need to clearly state what I'm trying to do and that I am not challenging or shooting anyone down.

Don't leave it up to the reader to decide what your mood is. Often, they'll assume there is disappointment or frustration when maybe there is none. I learned early on that my emails wouldn't contain my natural voice inflections to let people know when I was brainstorming versus giving a directive, so I had to learn how to be clear and let the reader in on those motives. This made me a better communicator as it did not leave anything up for interpretation but rather was made crystal clear.

The discernment for when an actual conversation needs to take place is something that is lost in today's technological workplace. If an email chain goes back and forth more than twice on a single topic, I implore you to pick up the phone. You might think email is more efficient, however, what I have found is that if both parties are not super clear in their email communication, this is far from an efficient form of having the discussion. If you sense misinterpretations or offenses are happening, do not continue to email but choose to call. Oftentimes the tone of your voice adds clarity, and you can end up solving whatever the issue is quickly.

BODY LANGUAGE

One of the most impactful lessons I have learned was about my body language. I had just joined a small group of restaurants as a new General Manager. I was intimidated by this group, as they had worked together for a while and seemed to get along well. At my first General Manager meeting, all eight of us sat around a big round table for our monthly meeting. I was a bundle of nerves, hoping nobody would notice me and that I would not embarrass myself. I had a huge case of imposter syndrome going on. I listened and followed along, thinking it was a good meeting but was relieved once it was over. Afterward, my Distract Manager pulled me to the side and asked me what my problem was. I was thrown by this question. What did he mean?! I didn't have a problem at all! He then informed me that I sat back through the entire meeting with my eyebrow up, frown on my face, and arms crossed over my body. He stated it looked like I did not want to be there and gave the impression that I thought they were not worth my time. I was mortified! This was not at all how I felt, and I was so very embarrassed I had come across like that. My body had told the opposite of how I felt.

From that moment on, I started realizing how I presented to others was within my control, and it was important I took control of the narrative. I began to understand that how I felt might not be naturally reflected by my body language. I needed to pay attention and manage it. You will not ever find me with my arms folded while at a professional event. I now understand this means "Do not approach," which is not how I want to be viewed. I have learned that when my eyebrow is raised (something it does very naturally) I am viewed to be mad or angry. Again, not what I typically want to communicate. So, now I scan my body. I ask myself "What's your eyebrow doing? Where are your shoulders? What are your hands communicating at this moment?" I reset when I notice my shoulders are up around my ears, or my eyebrow is sky-high. I sit forward a bit to ensure the person who is talking understands that I am listening. I make eye contact to send the clear signal that the other person is important and I hear/ see them. Without these self-scans, I am sure I'd be sending signals to others that aren't in line with my intentions or my true feelings.

> *We want to make sure what we are communicating, through all channels, is how we really feel. We want to ensure our body language is not communicating something different from our true intentions.*

What are some of your go-to body language signals that might need to be addressed?

- Do you point your finger at others while talking?

- Do you tend to use your hands a lot?

- Do you tend to sit with your arms crossed?

If so, could this come off as intimidating to others? It may be helpful to ask someone to record you having a conversation to see how your body is communicating. You could also ask someone you trust to give you feedback on your body language. Being mindful of how you communicate with your face and body is helpful to ensure your message gets heard. You're in control of how you communicate, whether it is verbally or non-verbally. Making sure your communication matches your intentions is key to effective communication.

I sometimes wish we were all constantly on camera with the ability to replay moments to gain insight. I would bet some of us would be shocked as to what we might see. The meeting that we didn't want to be in, how did we present ourselves?

The conversation that we thought we kept our cool in, how were our facial muscles presenting ourselves to the group? Our face and body language are constantly speaking to those around us, often without us knowing. People can signal they're upset or angry without ever opening their mouths. How? Because their energy and body language are letting others know what they are feeling, sometimes very "loudly."

While in human resources, a general manager, Tim, called me one afternoon to ask for help with an employee on his team. He let me know the employee had an outburst while at work and that he had a conversation with her. He felt their conversation went well, however, at the end of the conversation, she asked for a separate meeting with HR involved. I asked him where he was when he had this conversation, and he let me know that he was in a location where a security camera was. I asked him to give me fifteen minutes to call him back. I then proceeded to find the recording during the time he had told me the conversation had taken place. I was shocked at what I saw.

Tim was a kind and thoughtful person. He was typically quiet, not one to get loud or say things in anger. What I saw on tape, without audio, did not represent Tim in the way I had known him at all. What I saw was a larger man sitting with a smaller woman. I saw that the woman had her arms crossed tightly around her body, with her head down and not making eye contact. I saw that she had worked herself into the corner, physically seemingly to put as much distance between them as possible. I saw him sitting very tall almost leaning over her. He used his hands constantly, in what appeared to be a physically intimidating way. As she scrunched herself more and more into the corner, he grew taller and leaned more into her space. I stopped the video, appalled as to how this conversation had gone.

Let me be clear: I did not hear anything that was said. Tim could've used the best language possible. Tim could've been praising with his words. Tim could have said everything right. But what was wrong, Tim's body language, overshadowed every-thing else. I called Tim back and asked if we could meet. When we sat down together, I showed Tim the video of the conversation. Tim was shocked. He immediately started to explain everything he had said to her. He got defensive realizing that his body language looked like he was also using poor use of word choice. I let the video continue to play. Tim got quiet. Watching his actions on video helped him realize how important body language was. He made her feel unsafe; he made her feel unheard. He intended to have a great conversation; however, he allowed his body language to derail his intentions. He did not check in with himself to see how he was managing his emotions through body language, and he failed to check in with her to understand how she was feeling. He simply chose to react with emotion rather than to lead by example.

After we had a group mediation session where Tim was able to apologize and his employee was able to explain her feelings, we were then able to get to the root of the issue. Afterward, Tim let me know what an impact the video had. I can imagine the images he saw will be ones he recalls often in conversations going forward, and I am hopeful he's learned how important his body language is to achieve his overall goals.

Being mindful and checking in with your body language is helpful when talking with anyone, but essential in a difficult conversation. Like the story I shared about Tim, how would a conversation that you are having be viewed without sound? This should be a check-in point for you to make sure you're managing it well and that it's in line with your intentions.

SPATIAL AWARENESS

Taking your size into consideration is important. If you are a larger person, being in command of your body to ensure you are not towering over another as to not intimidate is essential. If you are smaller in size, sitting crouched in the corner will not set you up for a position of confidence in a conversation.

Checking in with our conversation partner is also important to ensure we are reading them correctly and responding accordingly. If you notice them slouching or sitting back with their arms crossed, simply ask why out of curiosity. If they are leaning over you, then also ask if they are aware of it. Like Tim, many may not be aware of how they are coming across with their body language. You bringing attention to this might be very helpful in the moment.

PAY ATTENTION

Dealing with difficult conversations means you need to not only be aware of the words being used but also the energy around you. When you do not pay attention to energy, or even worse, when you ignore it, you will only have a bigger problem later on to deal with.

I received a call one day when I worked in human resources to inform me that two employees got into a physical altercation while at work. This had taken place during a very busy lunch, in full view of at least 100 guests. The District Manager, John, informed me that the General Manager, Steve, was out of town on vacation. I proceeded with my investigation, which unfortunately led to the termination of both employees. When Steve returned from vacation, we sat down as a management team to review the situation. When asked if these two employees had an issue before this event, Steve informed me that he noticed there was tension between these two whenever they worked together, so he often had them on separate shifts. Steve never asked them what the issue was, let any of his other managers know there was an issue, or speak about this feeling to anyone. He simply noticed there was a problem, assumed the reason why, and went ahead with the remedy he came up with on his own. Since no one knew there was an issue, these two employees eventually worked together while Steve was on vacation, which led to a physical altercation. How could this entire situation have been avoided? What if Steve sat down with each employee as soon as he noticed the tension to ask about the situation?

The issue might have needed to be talked through and possibly could have been dealt with immediately. By avoiding the conversation, he created a situation which led each employee to take steps on their own resulting in the loss of their jobs, not to mention many guests in the restaurant witnessing the altercation and leaving with a bad impression of our company and our brand. By not acknowledging the reality and asking questions out of curiosity, Steve let down his entire team.

As a leader, when you witness or sense tension or possible arguments between your team members, it's your responsibility to address the issue by getting curious and seek to resolve the potential conflict prior to it getting out of hand and affecting the safety and care of the rest of your team.

RELATABILITY

We've previously touched on why admitting our mistakes and sharing with our team is important to building trust and connection. Relating to others' experiences is also helpful when speaking with employees, as they can see how you've overcome issues they might be struggling with. This allows you to be on the same team and see each other as works-in-progress, which is essential to having great teamwork in any field.

I have probably told the story of my body language lessons from my first General Manager meeting at least a thousand times by now. I typically use it when speaking to someone about their energy or attitude while at work. I tell it because I can relate to what they are going through, and I know how it feels to not be communicating with my body the way I think I am. I know the surprise when someone tells you that your energy is off. I know the moment of embarrassment to find out that what you are saying with your body language is opposite from how you want others to view you.

I've never told the story and not had an amazing but difficult conversation. We all have moments where we are surprised to find that we have a weak spot which needs to be worked on. It eases the pain when others share how they can relate to you in your embarrassment or pain. What have been your weak spots? When have you failed in a moment, and what learning points did you take away from that moment? What have you been able to overcome? These moments could be great learning lessons for others and could be used to find common ground with your employees and peers.

Is it uncomfortable to tell on yourself? Yes! We all want to look like we magically have it all together and have never stumbled once in our professional life. But this is just not the truth of it. We are human. We have made mistakes; however, those mistakes have allowed us to grow. We've all overcome unique obstacles and have worked hard to be where we are now.

I challenge you to get comfortable with being vulnerable by sharing how you can relate to the missteps of your team. I have found that each time I've shared in this way, I have been rewarded with the other person's trust and vulnerability. I have found they have accepted my challenges and have been able to overcome their own obstacles as well.

In the end, we all want the real human moments of connection, and we cannot get there without being a tad vulnerable. I invite you to sit down and recall those hard moments. Write them down and get comfortable with them. These will be useful tools for you if you are strong enough to be vulnerable with others and share these moments of learning.

Chapter Eight

Creating Success

"The single biggest problem in communication is the
illusion that it has taken place."
– George Bernard Shaw[11]

Questions vs Assumptions

During my time in human resources, I often followed up on conversations to find out that there were many assumptions made because there were not enough questions asked. When others are being told what to do rather than invited into a discussion, assumptions are made, and the end goal will not be reached. Even if the topic is around a policy which will not be changing, telling someone what the policy is and not discussing it might lead to an unfavorable end result. When we get curious and ask questions without judgments, we create a space for discussion to take place. When we allow our assumptions to lead the way or leave room for others' assumptions to fester, we are only delaying a larger conversation that needs to happen.

Sadly, if the larger conversations do not happen, the employees will not stay around for too long. I would challenge that even if you wouldn't mind if the person you are talking with decides to quit, there is a better way to reach that conclusion with them. Choose the path of discussion based on curiosity. If the

---

[11] https://www.brainyquote.com/quotes/george_bernard_shaw_385438

employee feels the same way after a discussion, you have led with integrity and both parties will walk away from the discussion with less resentment.

A good leader, whether a leader of one or a thousand, will be curious as to the other's experience, and will look to discuss *with* rather than talk *at*. Questioning with curiosity and without judgment will not only allow you to have a proper discussion but will open up other issues, suggestions, and learning opportunities for you. Many times, these learning opportunities come from discussions you wouldn't have expected them to.

I was able to mediate a conversation with a small team where the Director, Seth, had a conversation previously with his team in which he led with assumptions. Instead of asking why a project did not go according to plan, he started with the assumption that his team just didn't want to work the necessary hours for the project to be done right. When we restarted the conversation, removing assumptions and inserting questions without judgment, we found out that Seth had mistakenly skipped many crucial steps when laying out the project scope. During the original conversation, his team sensed his anger and energy and did not feel comfortable pointing out this issue. Since Seth led with assumptions, the team felt deflated and that their words or feelings did not matter, so no one felt the need to speak up.

When we were able to reset, get curious, and ask questions seeking to learn, we were able to brainstorm on the project scope, reset the expectations, and carry forward in a way which worked for all. Since everyone had an opportunity to point out what they felt was needed for this project to be done well, they had buy-in and were able to hold each other accountable. While the project was ultimately successful, Seth had some internal cleanup to do as his team felt a lack of trust after he led with his assumptions.

I find the phrases "Could it be true?" or "Have you considered?" help verbalize some of my thoughts, but I use these only after I ask general questions. These phrases are helpful when I'm sensing something hasn't been said and am trying to give space to those feelings and thoughts. When stating these phrases, I'm giving credence to the fact that I could be wrong and giving them a clear opportunity to correct me. This allows us to avoid assumptions entirely and get to the root issue at hand.

IS IT ME?

When I've made room for the possibility that maybe I've done something that might have upset another person, and even led with this possibility, it has often done wonders to start the conversation off in a way that does not position the other to be defensive. More often than not, I've been allowed to correct some of their assumptions, clarify my position, and come away with a new ally.

I remember when I started working with someone new and I got the feeling that she did not like me. In meetings, she'd often roll her eyes when I was talking. She seemed to take everything I said as a personal challenge to her. I sat with this feeling for two weeks, trying to figure out if I was being too sensitive or not. At the end of the second week, I decided I needed to address this, as it was still bothering me. I started by stating how I felt. I let her know I had noticed that she would roll her eyes in meetings when I talked, and I was wondering if I had maybe done something to her unintentionally. I let her know this had made me weary to share or open up, as I was afraid that there was something I had done to upset her, and I didn't want to further upset her. I told her the impact was that I didn't feel like we were true teammates.

She was surprised to hear this and let me know that she was slightly intimidated by me and was under the impression that I didn't like her! The eye rolls were not at me, per se, but rather at the history behind the ideas I had brought up. Apparently, there were several ideas I had brought up to the group that she had previously shared with ownership which were rebuffed. She apologized and let me know that this behavior and energy was not directed at me. We were able to talk through how we could be allies for each other, and how we needed the other to show up to be our best selves. I know without a shadow of a doubt that had I come to her with only assumptions and not questions born out of curiosity, the conversation would have gone very differently.

Sometimes we must consider that there are more reasons behind behavior than what we already know, and we need to give space to learn more about the situation without our judgments and assumptions getting in the way. When we do this, we may be surprised at the results.

RESOLUTION AND COMMITMENT

Finding a way forward means figuring out a solution both parties can agree to as well as commit to. This is key to having a successful conversation. Making sure there is a solution and commitment enables the other person, again, whether it is subordinate, peer, or sometimes supervisor, know that you are in this together.

I have worked for individuals who were very open to finding a joint resolution, who understood that if it didn't work for me, ultimately, it wasn't going to work for them. My happiness was tied to their happiness and my commitment was tied to their success. This knowledge built an environment where I was much more comfortable coming to them before there was an actual problem. I came to them to seek best practices, their guidance, or to brainstorm any situation that was giving me problems. I would implore you to look at how you think about your team's happiness and realize that their satisfaction is directly linked to your success.

At times, it's not easy to see a solution. A great solution doesn't always make itself readily available to us. Sometimes, there needs to be more questions asked and brainstorming on both sides. You might find that you are in a conversation with a team member and their proposed solution is not realistic; however, it could be an excellent jumping-off point. Explain the restrictions you are working with that makes their solution not realistic. Then modify their suggestion a bit to deal with the realities and ask what their thoughts are. You both can talk through how it might work best for either side.

Using the example of a tardiness issue, you could state that you would love to be able to allow them to come in later, however, office policy dictates a 9 A.M. start time. What is a possible solution? Maybe a two-week grace period of coming in later is doable so they have time to resolve a personal issue.

If you are dealing with peers or a different department not privy to your platform, systems, and processes you work with, you might have to educate them on the parameters of the situation. I suggest doing this in a tone that is not one of "That doesn't work for me" but rather, "I would love to tell you about what we are working with here." Give room to the possibility that you may have a blind spot, and work as a unit to get to a realistic solution.

Sometimes the solution is evident. If you're dealing with a tardiness issue, you may find that a schedule change would be possible and help an employee get to work on time. Even if the solution is relatively easy to agree upon, a stated commitment is also needed. This may sound something like "Going forward, I'll schedule you for 8 A.M. instead of 7 A.M. if you can promise me that you'll be in before 8 A.M. to be ready to work right on time. I'll also need you to commit to coming to me with issues before they become problems so we can work together to find a solution."

By agreeing to not only a solution but also getting a commit-ment to the solution, an expectation is made very clear and your team knows you are on their side and there to support them, but that you will also be holding them accountable. They will understand you have an interest in seeing them succeed. This is a much different conclusion to the conversation than if you simply inform and direct. A conversation which seeks engagement, mutually agreed-upon solutions, and commitments leaves a much stronger impact of support and connection.

CONTAGIOUS POSITIVITY

By nature, it's contagious when you show empathy and kindness to others. You make it easier for others to show empathy and kindness to you when you lead by example. It is quite a beautiful thing to see when a team functions from this premise.

When you start implementing the tools and foundational principles discussed in this book with your team, you will see how they will reflect your leadership style and also communicate with each other using these same principles themselves. You don't live in a vacuum. These values and intentional habits will get easier to implement because your team and your coworkers will be positively influenced by your habits and reciprocate by treating you with the same kindness, compassion, and appreciation.

It is a win-win for all and is not just about you. By developing your leadership skills, you are developing your team as well. Your employee retention and happiness will increase, and your team will thrive!

CHAPTER NINE

CONCLUDING THE CONVERSATION

Before ending the conversation, check-in to see if everything has been addressed that needs to be. Giving this moment to ensure all issues have been dealt with is valuable. You may feel everything has been addressed, however, they may have a feeling or thought not yet tackled. If they do not feel that everything was addressed, then the conversation is not over. Make the time. I promise your team is worth that investment.

ACKNOWLEDGMENT

I always thank people for taking the time to speak with me, even if I am their supervisor and they didn't really get a choice in the matter. It's still something that I want to make sure I say and hold for a moment. "Thank you for taking this time to speak with me," "Thank you for opening up," or "Thank you for sharing and for being vulnerable." Just saying those words carries so much weight. The simple acknowledgment and sharing of your feelings towards them can inspire reciprocation of trust and appreciation for you and your leadership. How many times have you been told today that your time and help is appreciated? I am going to guess not many, if at all. If somebody did tell you that, how would it make you feel? Probably pretty good. What will your feelings be the next time they want to talk? Will you dread it? Even if it's a hard conversation, by ending it with appreciation, you're probably going to have at least mediocre feelings around having a conversation again; the prospect of another conversation won't be upsetting. When you give appreciation, you are not only affecting someone at that moment, but you are also depositing into that goodwill bank that we spoke about previously. Don't forget to acknowledge and appreciate them and their commitment.

It's hard to be vulnerable. It is not easy to be open and trusting, especially with someone you may not have a history with. It's also hard work to dig into what's going on, why behavior has been what it is, and find resolutions that work. It is not easy. It takes mental energy and emotional energy, so appreciate it when your team puts in this hard work.

Another tool of communication is to appreciate in advance the commitment to enacting the solution. Encourage your team member by telling them how much you know they'll rock at their end of the solution. Let them know they can be successful in whatever it is you decided upon. Letting people know that you see them and appreciate them plus that you believe in their ability to be successful can pay huge dividends for all involved.

CONFIDENTIALITY

Keep confidentiality to build trust. I've seen some amazing conversations be undone in a heartbeat when the employee walks away, and a coworker comes up to the supervisor to ask what the conversation was about. Far too often, the supervisor will then tell everything that was just said, starting the not so fun rumor mill in the office or the restaurant. You might think you're building a relationship with the coworker you spill the beans to, but you are actually telling them they can't trust you to keep confidentiality. They might have their curiosity satisfied but will they feel comfortable coming to you with their own issues? Or will they hesitate, knowing you might be quick to speak to others about it?

By not keeping conversations confidential, or as confidential as possible, you will make your job a lot harder in the long run. To build trust with anyone, they must see you as having the skills to keep personal issues personal. While you may need to share details of conversations with critical people, check-in with yourself to ensure that it is absolutely needed, and you are not breaking the confidence and trust others give you.

FOLLOW UP AND ACCOUNTABILITY

The next step is the follow-up. If we promise to do something, set a calendar reminder, write a note to yourself, or send yourself an email reminder to complete what you promised you would do. If you expect them to take their commitment seriously, you need to give it that importance as well. It would be such a waste to go through a full conversation, connecting and building trust, only to not follow up and complete what you promised. The quickest way to destroy that freshly built trust is to not follow through on your commitment. Following up is important to ensure the change you are seeking takes place. This follow-up includes holding the other accountable for the commitments they agreed to as well as taking ownership of what you promised to do as well. Making sure that all know how to hold each other accountable and how to point out unhealthy behavior is crucial for a cohesive team to function long term.

THE IMAGINARY JACKET

One example of how I have used accountability is as follows. A common issue I have seen, especially in restaurants, is the energy level of an employee. Because you are dealing with guests all day, your energy needs to be upbeat throughout a shift, as the guest feels this, and service is affected. Energy from the staff is crucial to guaranteeing a great guest experience. If a team member is having a really bad day, unfortunately, that can be quite contagious to other team members and will influence the guest experience.

While this is a common issue, this is a subject that most feel uncomfortable tackling. I have had many conversations with employees in the service industry about the energy they bring into work. Sometimes we will come up with creative solutions to try to be more mindful of our energy when we walk in.

When I was a restaurant manager, I came up with a solution to this problem with one employee, Tammy. The solution we decided upon was to pause a moment outside the restaurant before her shift, take some deep breaths, and unzip an imaginary jacket. She agreed to go through the motions of unzipping this pretend jacket, which would signify all her burdens and responsibilities outside of work, and mimic taking off this jacket. We agreed that by physically going through this exercise, her brain would be signaled into another energy dynamic. This was going to help her to reset her energy and come into the restaurant with positivity and enthusiasm so she could impact her team in an uplifting way. We talked about how we were going to hold each other accountable by calling attention to the energy level with the word "jacket." If she came in and seemed to have forgotten to do this exercise, because she was running late or distracted, and therefore had low or negative energy, we agreed that I'd remind her about this commitment by simply saying "jacket."

A couple of weeks after we had this conversation, she entered the restaurant in a horrible mood. I didn't need to have a huge sit-down conversation with her. We didn't have to rehash anything. I just said, "Hey… jacket." Without missing a beat, she replied "Gotcha." She did a reset and you could see her kind of shake it off. Then her energy was right back up. This was awesome to see. Of course, I appreciated her in the moment. I said, "Tammy, thank you so much for that reset!" You could see that she appreciated the acknowledgment, then went on with her duties.

What would have happened if we did not come to the commitment to hold each other accountable? I am sure I might have gotten aggravated that she had poor energy after our previous conversation. I might've even sat down with her yet again, which I am sure would have been a much longer conversation. She may have felt like I was picking on her, and if she had had a bad day outside of work, might have reacted poorly to the conversation. We were able to avoid all of that because we had committed to holding each other accountable and agreed on how that would be done.

By simply using the one word that we committed to, she didn't feel as though I was picking on her or nagging her. She took it as a simple request to reset. That one word drew her attention to her energy, and she was able to make the change needed for a great shift. I would guess she probably felt like she mattered that day because I did not sweep it under the rug. I didn't ignore it. I held her accountable. I know that when I am held accountable for promises I make, I feel seen. I feel like I matter because somebody took a moment to remind me of what we agreed on.

As with everything, this goes both ways. When I let my team know that they could hold me accountable too, and we got clear as to how this would look or sound, it paid off in a big way with building trust and staying on the same page.

WHEN YOU FAIL TO FOLLOW THROUGH

Show respect to others by utilizing whatever tools you have at your disposal to help you follow through on the commitments you have made. But we need to acknowledge that we are human. You are going to mess up. Your subordinates, your colleagues or peers, your supervisor, and your boss are going to make mistakes and possibly not follow through with their side of the commitment. This is a guarantee because we are human. When the time comes that you do not uphold a commitment for whatever reason, acknowledge it. Don't be defensive. Don't be bashful, but instead, fully own it. Lead by example. Again, you must hold yourself accountable before you can hold anybody else accountable.

If you promise to schedule somebody thirty hours, and two weeks later you completely forget and schedule them for twenty hours and they bring it up to you, apologize. Acknowledge that you failed to uphold the commitment you made with them. When we do this, we show by example how we want our team to react to mistakes as well.

This means that we can't take it personally when others make mistakes, because it's not about you. Take it for what it is. They are human. It could simply be a human error. As I've said before, I truly believe that no one goes to work every day with the intention of doing a bad job. It is incumbent upon us, as leaders, to point out mistakes, train or teach so those mistakes don't happen again, and follow up on holding each other accountable to ensure full teamwork going forward.

CHAPTER TEN

COMMON CONVERSATIONS

Throughout my career there are themes of conversations I have witnessed or have been a part of that came up repeatedly. I want to share these here for you, as I find that sharing best practices as well as how these conversations can go sideways can be helpful.

PIVOTING ON A PROJECT

A common issue I have seen is when a leader of a department decides to pivot or change direction on a project. Could be due to budget issues or possibly senior leadership has changed the timeline or scope of a project for good reason. How this change is proposed to the team is key to ensuring success. When the leader in question explains the situation then asks for opinions and thoughts of the team and truly listens, amazing things can happen.

On the other hand, when the leader simply tells the team that there needs to be a pivot but doesn't give space to hear out the issues or problems the team feels could impact the project, then the results aren't nearly as great, or worse yet, some team members may end up feeling so disengaged that they end up actively working against you. As leaders, it's tempting to want to state the change and expect the team to just get on board. But giving some time to hear out the team's thoughts, fears, and frustrations is a crucial step to having a cohesive team built on trust.

Often the first mistake leaders make out of the gate is not acknowledging how hard change is. As humans, most of us HATE change. We are typically creatures of habit. Not only that, but it takes a lot to get into the middle of a project or way of doing things, then have to pivot our mindset and actions. When someone comes in and wants to change things up, our automatic response is to resist. Knowing this and acknowledging it are imperative to get buy-in.

I have a friend, Jerry, who runs a café for a large organization. He is brilliant at his job, his team loves him, and he is adored by his guests. He is a star in the organization. He recently was put under a new Vice President to report to. This VP came in one day and told Jerry to change the way the merchandise was laid out.

The VP did not ask questions, didn't try to get feedback, or even have a conversation; he just gave his directives and left.

Now, Jerry is a seasoned leader, and while he was upset with the approach, understood that it had very little to do with him and it was all about the ego of the VP. So, he made the changes. The next week, the VP came in and let Jerry know that Corporate leadership decided to go back to the original way the merchandise was showcased. He did not apologize nor explain why either change was implemented at all; he just said to change it all back. Jerry had spent six hours on his day off to make the original change and was now thinking about how he would have to stay very late into the night to change everything back. On his way out, his VP told him to text him a picture after he was done. So, on top of everything else, he made Jerry feel he was not trustworthy. Jerry was livid.

What could have been handled differently? First off, the VP could have had a basic human conversation with Jerry to find out why the merchandise was laid out the way it was, what he thought about the current layout, and what Jerry felt could be done better. Then, he could have let Jerry know the change he was told to relay and why they wanted a change. The VP could have acknowledged this would be a lot of work and ask how he could be a resource to support him. He also could have talked through any challenges to relieve pain points. When the decision was then made to change it back to the original state, there should have been an acknowledgment of how much work it took and maybe even just a human moment about how much it sucked to have to redo everything. There could've been a bonding moment of just commiserating.

The VP could have let Jerry know why the decision was made to go back to the original way and talked through how this could be avoided in the future. If a picture were needed to show the VP's boss, this could have been explained to Jerry as well so that it was communicated that the new VP was not distrusting Jerry but simply following his boss' directions.

The WHYs are so important, and when explained, lead to a better understanding of the overall goal for everyone. It empowers people to bring their best every day because they are in on the plan. They know why they need to pivot to meet the end goal of the team. This could have been the start of a great working relationship where communication was valued, and dialogue was deemed important. Instead, Jerry became disengaged. Luckily and maybe not surprisingly, this VP was not there for long. Maybe this experience is a clue as to why.

Another common change is a change in the scope or timeline of a project. It's quite common for a team to be working hard on a project with a given timeline or objective and changes arise. Maybe it is a budgeting issue or because the company must respond to outside interests. The project might have to be sped up or delayed. How we convey this to our team is important not only for overall morale but also for engagement.

We do not want our team to be so disenfranchised that they end up not giving their all to the project. So, how do we go about this? First, I recommend acknowledging the obvious about the change which is that, oftentimes, it sucks and is hard. Allowing your team to have a moment to lament this fact is helpful. Explaining why the change must take place is also key. They might not be privy to the fact that you are not in full control of all aspects. They might assume that you have control over all changes decided upon, however, letting them know there are a lot of other factors that go into the project is important. Giving a glimpse at the bigger picture has always been helpful for me when explaining changes.

Then, open the discussion up to the team for input about what might need to be considered or how they think the best course of action moving forward is. It is important to hear from everyone in the group, which may mean you call out some people who are not quick to contribute. Getting each unique perspective is important to know how this pivot affects everyone's job as well as how they are all feeling about it. Often this step is overlooked or intentionally ignored, as the leader does not want to get stuck in a venting situation. Many leaders believe that there is not much use in this step. I disagree.

The team *will* be venting about this. You can choose to be included and help close the loop into a solution or you can choose to let the group do this without you, where it might devolve into lost support for the project. This decision is up to you. Personally, I like to be present to help focus on solutions and action while listening for learning opportunities.

Come to an agreement on how to move forward as a group as well as what each team member is responsible for. This helps ensure the project gets completed with the new scope or the new timeline. Try to talk through everything you can at this time, not leaving anything to fester.

Sometimes I've seen this process split in two parts. The first part could be the "pity" session if you will, where you let people vent and commiserate. You might want to use this session to lay out all the factors at play and what the bigger picture is. End this session with a rallying cry to come up with ideas on how to move forward, giving them all time to sit with this new information and brainstorm possibilities for the next meeting. The second session could then be to work on what is possible, what is doable, and a plan forward. With each session, it is important to hear from all and make sure that all thoughts are communicated before leaving the room. It has been my experience that if this does not happen, those unsaid feelings and thoughts will fester and cause issues down the road.

Be a Resource

Being a resource who is open to brainstorming is key when things change. Again, be ready for the pushback. This should be expected. Once you get past this, help your team think about what is possible.

Brainstorming out of the box possibilities is hard for many. So many have their brains set to how things typically happen and what has worked in the past and cannot see a new way to do something. This is where we can shine as leaders!

I remember working with a team that had to get reports out by a certain time every week. This deadline had been set in stone for years, however, the leadership team had decided that to help make better decisions, the reports were needed earlier. This was met with a hard "no" from each team member. I was brought in to help them get to a point of "yes." The first thing we did was brainstorm about what was possible. I asked them to think about possible solutions if they had an unlimited budget and resources. This question is meant to inspire big and out of the box ideas. I asked them to throw out everything they had thought about these reports and to envision starting from the ground up. After gathering the out of the box ideas, we discussed the constraints that we were dealing with to come up with the best possible solutions.

We ended up implementing two different systems which not only got the information needed to create the reports earlier but aided in their data entry of this information. They were able to get reports out much earlier than previously thought, and the leadership team was happy. The team simply needed someone to help think through what could be possible and be given permission to get creative with solutions that might work. When I have first questioned what is possible with unlimited time and resources, it is amazing what out of the box ideas come forward!

WHEN YOU DON'T HAVE ALL THE INFORMATION

What to do if you are a director or a supervisor and you've gotten word the project scope has changed, but that's all you've been told? Maybe it started with a nine-month timeline and now has been shrunk to four months. Or maybe the marketing plan your team has been working towards has now been directed to be changed? You are responsible for notifying your team of the changes. So, what do you do if you don't have all the "why" information? Ask for it!

I suggest going to your leader and asking why this change is needed. And again, I would recommend leading with your intentions. State that you are not there to challenge or argue the point, but to collect as much information as possible to help your team reach the end goal the company has set. Sometimes, they may not have these answers and need to go seek them out themselves. Request they get the information so that you can help your team be on the same page as the company. Without knowing the why, it is harder to be successful.

Remember your goal is to seek out answers to best support your team and the company. Your number one responsibility is to ensure your team feels protected and safe. To do this, you cannot just be a robot and pass on small pieces of information. You have a responsibility to pass on as much information as possible.

Understanding what additional resources are available is also useful information to have before communicating a pivot or change to your team. Is overtime possible/approved to get work done, if needed? Can additional people be added to the team? Do we need to consider outsourcing a part of the project? All of these should be considered; however, these ideas might not appear until you brainstorm with your team. Again, this is why you are in the leadership position, to help your team come up with creative solutions and motivate them to complete the project. It is amazing what people can do if they feel supported and appreciated and if they feel like their supervisors are invested in the success of the whole team.

FAVORITISM

A complaint that comes up a lot is favoritism. Unfortunately, most of the time, managers avoid this conversation to their detriment. Often, this issue comes up when you are dealing with something else entirely. You may be talking about a performance issue, and the charge of favoritism is leveled at you. Or, you may be giving feedback, and a snide remark is made about "one of your favorites." To simply brush off these comments will only hurt your reputation and will not help you build up trust with your team. Dealing with this head-on will allow you to possibly learn and/or reset expectations.

Take the example of a General Manager I once worked with, Gary. Gary tried to accommodate the schedule requests of his staff whenever possible. One of his employees, Sam, was constantly getting schedule requests in late, and typically, was not accommodated because of the tardiness of the requests. This eventually led to a very disengaged employee who did not feel valued. The issue came to a head one day when Gary was giving feedback on the performance, letting Sam know he was not completing tasks before moving onto new tasks. Sam got so worked up, that he ended up yelling at Gary in the middle of the kitchen. Gary was taken aback and asked to meet with Sam right then. When asked why there was an outburst, Sam angrily communicated how he felt there was favoritism. "You always give everyone else the days off they request, but not me! Then you come at me telling me I'm not working hard!" Gary could have taken this discussion in many different directions, however, he paused to deal with each part separately.

He calmly explained why some got schedule requests honored, and others didn't. He explained why the timing of request notices was so important, and the first-come, first-serve policy of requests meant that the sooner you got the request in, the better the chance of it being honored. He even pulled up the texts and emails he had received from Sam to show him how late his past requests had been.

Gary then dealt with the issue of feedback, stating the expectation for all team members was to fully complete a task before moving on to another task. Gary continued by letting Sam know he was very valued, that the team needed him, and that feedback was given only to make him better, not to tear him down. The conversation concluded with Gary and Sam agreeing that if there were any frustrations in the future, they would be brought up immediately and not be allowed to fester.

By not becoming defensive, Gary was able to listen and truly hear Sam. He was able to discuss the problem that had arisen and then, once the issue was resolved, Gary was able to communicate expectations so they were clear going forward. He was then able to let Sam know he was valued and that his feedback was welcomed. He did not lash out and mirror Sam's energy, he didn't try and dominate to show his authority, and he didn't brush the accusations under a rug. He calmly listened and addressed everything separately. The result was that Sam felt seen, heard, and valued.

Another example of how the issue of favoritism played out was when an employee, Dierdre, asked her Director, Suzanne, to help her understand a program a bit better. They agreed to set up some time during lunch once a week for a "training session." While this was an awesome idea, it was not communicated to others in the department. All they saw was one of their co-workers eating lunch with their Director once a week and assumed that they were now close friends. This led to frustrations rising, people seeing every remark made through this lens of "favoritism," and finally an outburst during a department meeting. This time, it wasn't handled in the best way. The frustration was mirrored back because Suzanne didn't believe she had done anything wrong. Instead of simply correcting the assumption and explaining to the team what was happening and how they misunderstood, she took the outburst as disrespectful and an affront to her leadership and reacted with frustration. Had she managed her ego and recognized that the feelings presented were valid however misguided, she could have corrected the assumptions and even offered to do training lunches with her other team members if they would like.

The key differences displayed in these two examples are the ability to separate ego from the conversation and knowing the difference between reality and perspective.

COMMUNICATION STRATEGY

Part of your job as a leader is to make sure work gets accomplished. This means that you must communicate with your team regarding their work to know if/when issues arise on various projects. You might also have people above you who need progress reports. Often issues arise based on how you have chosen to communicate with your employees regularly. Being kept in the loop is important for various reasons. We need to think about our communication strategy and we also need to discuss this strategy with our employees.

We are all unique and we have unique needs. Some work well autonomously, with little to no oversight. These individuals might be very put off if you want them to communicate with you throughout the day to update on projects. Others enjoy regular check-ins and additional communication and attention.

Choosing how you are going to manage people, without hearing how they wish to be managed, can lead to problems. I have seen people leave positions because the communication strategy in their department was not a fit, and often the supervisor had no clue that the problem was the way they communicated on a daily basis.

When I hire a new employee to work on my team, one of the first things we do is discuss a clear communication strategy. I ask how they wish to be communicated with, what they need in their communication from me, and conversely, what I need from them. Then we come up with a structure that works for both. The strategy might include weekly meetings to discuss projects or issues, giving the employee ample time to voice any concerns where they know they have my undivided attention. Or a strategy could utilize apps to manage projects and stay on the same page. Another idea might be daily, ten-minute calls to check-in and stay connected. You need to be in agreement after discussing needs and fears or concerns.

While working in Human Resources, I had an employee who came to me fearful that he was going to lose his job soon. When I asked why he thought this, as I knew the Director of his department was happy with his work, he stated it was because his Director checked in with him every morning. He assumed this was because the Director didn't trust him. This was incorrect. His

Director did not take the time to discuss a communication strategy. If he had, the employee would have known that the Director was the one who needed the daily morning check-ins. This was the Director's preferred way to know what was going on but not because trust was an issue. The lack of a discussion regarding this strategy led to the employee fearing an impending job loss.

Once we all sat down to discuss what each party's communication needs were and why, we could then come up with a strategy that worked for all. The employee was able to understand he was valued and that his work was appreciated. Going forward, this person understood why the check-ins were happening and did not assume the reason was a lack of trust. If this discussion about communication strategy had been done initially, then this trust misunderstanding and hurt feelings could have been avoided. The great part about this experience was that as different issues came up in this department, they were able to use this discussion as a template on how to resolve them.

Most leaders do not put much thought into their daily communication strategy. I hope I've given you some reasons to think about why you should give intentional thought and have discussions about what strategy is best for the unique needs of your team.

Chapter Eleven

Leading Your Team

Balance

The amount of patience needed to be an effective leader and a good communicator cannot be overstated. Often, I have leaders tell me they are just not patient people by nature. I quickly let them know that this might be an area to invest some time or resources in to improve, as I personally have never worked for someone I felt was a great leader who didn't also have the qualities of a patient person.

I've encountered so many people who have the vision, drive, and determination to do great things, however, have not discovered or acknowledged the need to build connections as a key factor of success. Many brilliant people have tunnel vision when it come to their goals, but if you don't connect with others and have the difficult conversations to meet your team's needs, your long-term success in any organization will be hindered. Now, this can be taken too far. I'm sure you have worked with someone who was the office or company gossip. This person was rarely seen working, and often seen talking with others about topics that had nothing to do with work. I find that extremes are never good. The balance of being focused and task-oriented, combined with time spent to connect with your team, is often the best approach. And when you take the time to connect, remember to keep it within appropriate topics.

It is a bit of a balancing game that good leaders know how to play. While completing your daily tasks, try to take some time to connect with others. This gives margin to have conversations that are needed when the energy is off, and it allows for some time to dig into the root causes of issues. This type of leadership can't happen when you are constantly functioning in a fire-fighting mode. If you remember from earlier in this book, fire-fighting mode is when you are running from one emergency to the other, not able to plan or anticipate because you and your team are pulling each other from one issue of urgency to another constantly. This usually happens when the leader is more comfortable working in a fast-paced chaotic environment. But this isn't good for team morale and doesn't create an atmosphere of trust and connection. The team will typically not have their leaders' full attention which is frustrating. If you find that this is the mode you usually work in, think about a new strategy and how to implement it.

CREATE A SAFE SPACE FOR OTHERS TO INITIATE DIFFICULT CONVERSATIONS

As Doris Kearns Goodwin, an esteemed American biographer and historian writes, *"Good leadership requires you to surround yourself with people and diverse perspectives who can disagree with you without the fear of retribution."*[12]

This means we need to invite people to challenge us and seek to enter into meaningful discussions with people who have different perspectives or points of view. The way that we do this

---

[12] https://pittsburghlectures.org/lectures/doris-kearns-goodwin/

is to create a safe space by not reacting out of ego or anger when difficult conversations are initiated by others. Often, we get feedback from our employees or peers in ways that might not sound kind. Maybe they have been wanting to challenge us on a project or way of thinking and have had to work up the courage to speak up. Sometimes this feedback is given in a rushed way and often in a moment that is supposed to be focused on something else entirely. How we react in the moment will either create more trust or will break down what little trust had been established. When we stop, welcome this feedback, and indicate we would like to discuss it at a more appropriate time, we let all present know that value feedback, welcome different viewpoints, and will make time to fully delve into the conversation.

This is a great way to encourage others in our team to have the courage to stand up to us as well, but hopefully, in a more appropriate time/place. If we shut down the conversation, then this sends a noticeably clear signal to others that we do not want to be called out on anything. The consequences of our actions will, unfortunately, be hard to undo.

I once worked for someone who loved discussing different perspectives, however, he had a very rigid view about when this should be done. If someone spoke up and he felt they were out of place, he would shut the conversation down hard. He did not explain that the feedback was wanted, but the timing or place was the issue. He just shut down any conversation about it. This indicated to his team that he did not want anyone else's opinion.

He was confused later as to why his team wasn't forthright when he sought out opinions. He couldn't understand the connection between these two events. He simply thought there was a time and place that feedback or differing opinions was appropriate and thought this was clear to his team. He never stated this but assumed his team understood his thought process. They did not. The team didn't feel comfortable speaking up, even in private, and this led to issues with team trust. These issues ended up having to be dealt with through very difficult conversations.

As a leader, what you do or say in every situation sends ripple effects through your team. When you are mindful and intentional in all interactions, you will signal to your team your desires for either their honesty with you or if you would like them to keep their opinions to themselves. The choice is yours.

When you engage with your co-workers, whether peers, subordinates, or supervisors, in a way which gives space for learning and revealing the root cause, we build space for honesty. When your conversations mostly involve giving directives, you do not build that space for honesty. Think about a time you had a leader or a manager who ruled with an iron fist. I am sure you can immediately picture somebody from your past, someone who possibly even said to you, "I'm the manager, I'm the supervisor – it's my way or the highway." Did this person make you feel comfortable to bring issues to them? Did they make you feel like you could point out a downside to any of their ideas? Probably not. You probably felt it was best to keep your head down and just do your work quickly and leave.

I am asking you to consider how your behavior during your interactions with your team makes them feel, and to take responsibility for that. Building a space for honesty is accomplished through every interaction you have. You cannot have it both ways. You will not build a safe space by bullying them in tough conversations. Every interaction you have is teaching those around you how you wish to be treated, how you wish to be seen, and what type of relationship you wish to have with them.

INVEST IN DEVELOPMENT

Developing out the competencies of being a great leader is a life-long process. Your development should never be stagnant. Always seek out opportunities and ways to strengthen your skills and develop your leadership understanding. While this book gives clear ways to improve communication with your team, peers, and supervisors, there is still much more you can do to grow your skillset as a leader. What development are you currently partaking in?

Development is different than training as development is typically transferable skills that are less tactical, while training is more task-oriented and tailored to the specific needs of your current position.

Do you know the areas you need to grow in? I hope some have become clear as you've read this book. What a great opportunity! Now you can develop a plan to attack these areas! Read more from leaders you respect. Have conversations with your team, supervisors, and mentors. I passionately believe in coaching as a wonderful way to assist in development. Coaching can help identify areas of improvement and growth opportunities. It can help you set goals and gives practical help by empowering you with the right tools to reach your goals!

Do you have a clear idea of your goals and how to work towards them? I would ask you to consider your development and your team's development as your number one priority, and not just the sole responsibility of the company you are working for. Put a plan together to ensure that you get the support you need.

Once you believe development is a personal priority and become serious about pursuing ways to grow, I promise you that the goals you set for yourself will truly be within your reach!

CPSIA information can be obtained
at www.ICGtesting.com
Printed in the USA
LVHW021828021220
673228LV00052B/2743